ENDER BAŞKAN

# TWO HUNDRED MILLION MUSKETEERS

NEW POEMS

First published 2025
from the Writing and Society Research Centre
at Western Sydney University
by the Giramondo Publishing Company
PO Box 557
Willoughby NSW 2068 Australia
www.giramondopublishing.com



Cover and design by Jenny Grigg
Typesetting by Andrew Davies
in 9/15 pt Tiempos Regular

Printed and bound by Pegasus Media & Logistics
Distributed in Australia by NewSouth Books

A catalogue record for this book is available from the
National Library of Australia.

ISBN: 978-1-923106-48-2



9 8 7 6 5 4 3 2 1

The Giramondo Publishing Company acknowledges the support of Western Sydney University in the implementation of its book publishing program.

This project has been assisted by the Commonwealth Government through Creative Australia, its arts funding and advisory body.

## Contents

## Here Is The Shirt, (Get) Off My Back / Swimming In The Afternoon

if you want an alarm clock to work
make sure you
place it out of reach
but never mind
our mutual friends are awake and so are we
549am
i am dad
im on demand
raaaah-biiiish truuuuuuck!
i run out to see the bin flung up and over
with you
why is the driver wearing sunglasses?
even if you miss the first truck
you get 2 more chances
sometimes a hot air balloon
milk! daddy can you make me a milk?
you fill the bottle / start the kettle / grind the coffee
rumi said you make your own oil as you cook
and as a cooker i say lets cook / crudely
the power of concentration
vis-á-vis
concentrations of power
the russians have the kremlin
the ottomans had the sublime porte
and both our children have runny noses
sometimes your bigness makes other people feel small
and sometimes your bigness makes other people feel bigger

we go away
we buy our friends gifts
wooden spoons and
knock-off footy shirts from the spice bazaar
we fly home long haul
gifts packed and wrapped
they live in coburg
us in brunswick east
the gifts sit in our drawers for months
the sky
    it reels
        with love
someone said his diaries were better than his novels
August 2nd 1914
kafka writes
*germany has declared war on russia – swimming in the afternoon*
praise be! praise be to allah! praise you like i should
all praise
all rights unreserved
all rise no judgement
ezgis first word is dudu
everything is dudu
dudu means thing
dudu dudu dudu
her sister is dudu
her second word is dede
third word mum
fourth word dada
fifth word woof

sixth word more
now every animal is woof
and now everything is more
every dudu is more
dudu dudu dudu
more more more
my pockets are filled with crumpled tissues and battered coins
and after doing the laundry and forgetting to check pockets
now all these clothes are flecked white
and i shake shake shake them and you know what
even dust is beautiful when the light hits
more more more more
a pocket call from dad
when sending letters and submitting poems via the post i use
reply paid envelopes i borrow from work the guy at the post
office says they wont arrive without a stamp
but they almost always do
someone at some depot
some worker some robot doing me a solid as i pick up our
doormat take a dozen steps into the garden and slap it
with a broom boom one two even after twenty slaps
it still explodes dust
and thats theory
against our better no judgement in that we beef with its aesthetics
my older daughter starts little athletics
saturday morning on the track i ran on as a kid
my parents take her / thanks mum n dad
one day they take her late its strategic so she misses long jump
and wont bring sand into their new car
she finishes last in all the running but makes friends

on the last meet of the season i finally make an appearance
wearing a big hat i found in lost property and sunglasses
a coffee cart here
a labor minister there
on the tongs behind the bbq
dad is it still a boycott if girls do it?
all the parents are doping
all the children are unclean
all the artists must suffer
and i wonder if losing if getting beat is good for you
now plunged into an abyss of middle-aged
left-wing melancholia to be recognised by prowling hyper-caffeinated
re-financed class-ascendant former schoolmates lucky my kid
is an anarcho-terrorist anti-capitalist critical-theorist
and disarms their line of enquiry with logic
calls them poo-poo heads...
later reflecting at a petrol pump for
4 cents off a litre i receive
another pocket call from dad
and thats dangerous too
another garbled voicemail
more more more more
i came last in all the races dad dilân says
yes you did i say and how does that make you feel?
i havent got any medals dad / do poets get medals dad?
only john ashbery nowadays
but poetry was at the olympics until 1952
until the olympics came to australia and we abolished it!
americas best-selling poet is a 13th-century sufi mystic
we call mevlana and you call rumi

my dad would work late in his home office
the anti-murnane
shredding documents constantly
keeping me up
demonstrating a work ethic
nowadays i write into the night
now i am reeling i am talking to my former schoolmate
for the sake of our children
i am swimming in the afternoon in the morning
i am handed a large latte i didnt ask for
but graciously accept
i never truly understood
coffee until i became a parent
and things like cross-fit and smoothies and waitlists
when i say coffee you say yes please
when i say poetry you say on your knees!
an old commo says to me so youre a man of the left huh?
and i say yeah what about you and he says
well im an eco-socialist with an anarchist heart
more more more more
daddy tissues! daddy tissues! dilân yells
as she licks a drip on her upper lip
later
i watch her play a game with her friends in the gaga-pit
called danger baby where they froth from the mouth
try not to drown
try not to get nits and i i i i at first i laugh
and then i break i tear up
cos as a parent
as a parent

as a parent
how do you
how do you
how do you
deal with a sober vision of this world
we go on
as grapes become wine capsicum becomes tear gas
and of all things to be afraid of im afraid of wanting to
take writing take language to its limit
but im afraid
so let me take a moment to quote june jordan
*if we lived in a democratic state our language would have*
*to hurtle, fly, curse, and sing, in all the common names, all*
*the undeniable and representative participating voices of*
*everybody here. we would not tolerate the language of the*
*powerful and, thereby, lose all respect for words... we would*
*make our language conform to the truth of our many selves and*
*we would make our language lead us into the equality of power*
*that a democratic state must represent.*
amen
poets gotta walk the walk
you gotta walk the tiger
sell the dummy
more more more more
a parent twice deep
down often but
up late and up early
i grab a tea towel to try to muffle the sound of the coffee grinder
so the others wont wake up not only for them but for me
cos damn i just need a little solitude

but the tea towel is not enough so
i take off my shirt and use that too
be prepared
if you have small children i recommend you carry tissues
bandaids / pencils / paper / pawpaw cream / liquid paracetamol
butter menthols
and fishermans friends on you at all times
and if you are at the deli you should take a number
and just meditate on the olives fetas and cold cuts
cos its a future and its a cheeseboard
more more more more more more more
somethings that arent punk that arent rocknroll might be
revolutionary
dudu
some nights i set up my aeropress for the morning
lay out my clothes n feel pleased
one night cleaning the house
i limit myself to putting away 449 objects
including pebbles of possum shit / rubber bands / wooden dolls and a
button called tracey and at dinner i ask a friend who
i collect rubbish with on the merri creek
if shes an eco-feminist
she laughs pauses says… i mean probably… are you?
we grew up in the 90s
she went to mittagundi
i went to the mcg
across the table our other friend scoffs
as an artist she says i dont subscribe to labels
daaaaaad dada dada dada
another pocket call from dad

most times i feel out of place
and most places i feel out of time
ddaaaaad i did a pooooooo! come!
everyone always expected more from me
more more more more
ezgi sees a bird and says woof woof
everything is entangled
everything is fungal
and emotions arent personal since they come from the outside...
another pocket call from dad
another 4 cents off a litre
of all places i am in gallipoli with a menacing headache and
the guy at the bus station makes me a
nescafé with four sugars and milk and prayer and puts me to sleep
and i owe my life to him
an hour and a half later im up
coffee baby
lets go! lets live! lets write about it
language is a bus / no / language is a mug / no / language is a dog
follow it stroke it play with it feed it sleep with it at your feet dont
buy insurance pick up the shit and pocket it
woof woof woof no
language is a big cat it cannot be contained
dilân swaggers into the kitchen after school while gabe is cooking
she says WHATS FOR DINNER BIGG BOIII?
and tea towel over his shoulder he beams hes floored
gabe is cooking doms chicken woof woof
which is really ellas chicken
but dom cooked it for gabe heaps
and made it his own woof woof woof

even though its ellas recipe though she too got it
or built it from somewhere and put it in her book
and now gabe opens up her book
and cooks it most mondays
and after he moves out i start cooking it
and call it gabes chicken...
bak bak bak
these traces these footnotes these contaminants!
in sydney theres asbestos in playground mulch
in turkey theres arsenic in the euphrates
in melbourne there r scraps of paper with literary value
left in my pocket and made soggy
by the machine
now tumbling down the sewers
maybe even hitting the creek
227am
daaaaad i weed the bed
shoehorns tunics fishing vests big hats sunglasses with side windows
lets enter the middle ages with aplomb
another pocket call from dad
more more more more
daaaaad
at an interview for a job in a café the owner is accompanied by their guru
who asks me
and how would you describe your relationship with your father?
daddy tissues daddy tissues! dilân yells
i reach into my pocket where theyve balled up
i unscrunch them and hand them over
eeeeehh ezgi writhes as
i wipe her nose

she cant talk much but she can really communicate
later i realise that its not having her nose wiped that she hates
but that i dont ask or that
i dont tell her what im doing cos damn shes a person
not a cute cutie so cute so cute thing
im not a
        im not a
                im not a
                        im not a
                                im not a
im not a dictator im a guide im a comrade
i have authority but im not an authoritarian
i am an author but what about...
just gonna pick you up now ezgi lets put some sunscreen on now
little one ok? here you go you put some on my face first
im just gonna put you down so i can change your nappy
im just gonna wipe your nose now ezgi
thats it im just gonna wipe your bum your
pooey bum is that ok baby?
here are my keys
i love you baby
i love you canım
from sophie i learn to talk i learn to narrate the action
to give a sense of knowing and calm to my children
and maybe to myself and to her...
this is what im doing im writing now reader
i go to al-alamy café to meet my friend and give him his gift
five months after we return
in some cultures if you compliment a person on a thing of theirs
they offer it to you there and then

hes a bosnian serb so i give it a go
put his gift / his soccer shirt on over mine
and go over to him
we hug and talk and he hasnt said anything about the shirt yet so
i stand up and say
hey i got you this shirt...
dilâns learning italian at school and now she can say things like
prego bella ciao and mettiti il cappello
which means put your hat on
but mornings we ride our bikes to school and say
mettiti l'elmetto and when we get to school mettiti il cappello
we end up talking with a parent who says oh how fun!
are your roots italian? id loooove 2 speak another language!
well i already know three languages dilân flexes
i know english turkish and another language that is very old!
we found it tucked under the world
and not many people speak it but me n my friend
dot found it and we speak it and my dad speaks a bit too
its called shuey-ma-shuey
and its tucked under the world!
the parent raised eyebrows smiles to me as if to say cute
but i refuse to collaborate
and what do you do she says
im a proud parent i say
my dads a poet! dilân yells
delivery!
the man steps in through the back door at work and asks / name?
he types in ANGER
initial? B
on the screen he waves in front of me i sign what it says

B.ANGER
banger
dudu dudu dudu
in 1828 the masters and servants act was passed in australia
aiming to quash the nascent workers movement / put people in their
place / reinforce the imposition of stolen land / free labour and
continuing genocide
after five or six hours of uninterrupted sleep sophie
rises and says... i feel a hundred dollars!
dictators are everywhere
i hate them
but its the imperialist bourgeoisie who are the real gangsters...
kafka writes on june 21st 1913
*the tremendous world i have in my head. but how to free myself and*
*free it without being torn to pieces*
whats your cancellation policy?
philosophy
bros before hoes
dasein before starsigns
and just a little housekeeping before we go on
for our sponsors funders and corporate partners
im not a political poet
im not a political animal
im not a political person
thank you very much
one of the recurring pieces of advice my labor-voting father gives me...
in life ender there are horses and there are jockeys
and you want to be a jockey
dont you mean bosses and workers dad?
ender its like this...

he butted heads with his bosses so he left and
started the same business
became self-employed
became his own jockey?
woof woof woof
here i am fighting my whole life just to use my name
refusing a coffee name
and then the brown delivery driver shows me how it is
name? any name will do! anger! banger! whatever
nom nom nom de plume
many of us come from dysfunctional families but all of us
live in a dysfunctional society
like people in richer cultures our friends name their kids after heroes
like curly and etel and frida and ursula
but we just went with feel and a little aesthetics
more more more more
i like wearing silk and i like sitting in saunas but
i dont wanna be a jockey and
i dont wanna be a broken-in horse either
i wanna be a bronco a mustang a brumby or
a wild horse among wild horses
unbroken and in revolt – RUN!
i say my new coffee name but it doesnt go down well
how do i spell that? shes poised with a pen
and i quote dilân – VKXQLBJD
shes learning to write and she doesnt know yet how many horizontal
lines go on the letter E
sometimes its four or six and the other day i counted nine lines
and i love that cos
i was told the poet is a sorcerer responsible only to animals

for those without a voice
how did people know to call dinosaurs dinosaurs? dilân asks
humans invent our languages sophie replies
a jaw-dropping moment for our daughter
so i can invent it?
you already have!
depending on how attuned you are shuey-ma-shuey might not appear to
have words like any other language but has worlds
pitterpatterbopbibop a childs free jazz...
dudu dudu dudu dudu
mettiti il cappello mettiti l'elmetto
mettiti il cappello mettiti l'elmetto
sophie and i spend the night together / early days
we wake up in her cramped but beautiful room in fitzroy north
2nd storey big window sun streaming in dust dancing / im so happy
and from silence my first words of the day
are you a communist?
i think so she says
and that my friends was all...
the conditions of entry at childcare include
no runny noses for 24hrs
i pull a tissue from my shirt sleeve as we approach the entry
ezgi can i wipe your nose baby?
myyeh eeeeh she refuses cos its her snot and she wants to glue it
across her cheeks and snail-streak her sleeves
they say the best way to stop a child from doing a thing you
dont want them to do like biting or eating their own boogers
is to explain your reasons and be firm and unemotional
dont make a big deal out of it...
the eco-socialist tells me he was toiling away

in little rock arkansas when his daughters friends dad
a third-way politician and sax player got a job in DC
tearing these friends apart...
upward mobility! will soon send you into orbit!
daddy tissues daddy tissues
im thirsty daddy! me too!
runny noses are banned at childcare
all the children at childcare have noses
and half of them are runny
systems at breaking point
viral and fiscal
an issue of liquidity
you are riding to school along the creek with your kids
and the neighbours kids
your little one in her seat and the five-year-old fanging it up
ahead with her best friend...
this is a flex
you are proud you taught her to ride without training wheels
ran alongside her with your hand on her back
no prangs just a couple of skinned knees and palms
sometimes your kid gets annoyed at you
cos you give too much advice
wrong tone like a dog owner youre not her owner
shes not your property
woof woof woof
but when she loses concentration you flinch
more more more
its visceral
she veers into the path of an oncoming $13,000 commuter bike
ridden by a manic lawyer

you try to chill / youre a poet
you bank on her survival instinct prevailing over her death drive
meanwhile you try to wipe ezgis nose before
the snot glues into evidence
sometimes you see other parents being tyrannical
and the only difference between you and them
is time and space and maybe breakfast
youve been there
you recall like a mantra that emotions arent personal cos
theyre from the outside
you reject a cool dad / bad dad binary
like you reject a rich dad / craw dad
but you have to say sometimes lets go! or come on!
or remembering that youre a poet and seeing the serpent sign along
the bushes say
youre swerving and slithering kids! no snakes on the road please!
and they laugh but they swerve anyway as we all go PASSING!
her nose gets itchy
and she slams the brakes
when im tailing her but
its still a beautiful scene and as
my friend gilles says you dont desire a woman you desire an ensemble
or you desire a landscape with a woman in it
which is to say you dont desire prosciutto but just an inner-city life
sitting in the sun with natty wine and friends eating off a cheeseboard
or depending on your own class consciousness
have a beer and a snag in sliced bread...
tinchi linchi kla haji anji inji ya
inji anji injia ya
klip klop

dip dop
dudu dudu dudu
its 1030pm after 12 years together
and youre tired youre wrecked and yet
all that desire is still palpable and i say to sophie
its not you! i love you! i just miss my friends my ensemble
if only we were part of a church wed be sorted
wed have a readymade community / friends / a canonical text
a time and place to meet up
mutual aid a historical mission
wed sing together and children would be welcome...
they say you need something to look forward to
one day ill be making pocket calls
642am
i walk over to the coffee grinder and fill it with beans
this morning ezgi has walked in and i sit her on the counter
grab a tea towel and she says
dudu dudu dudu... ehhhh ehhhh
as she pulls up her top / offering it to me...
in turkish
    the heart doesnt beat
        it throws

## A Workers Paradise

i go to work / i go to work / i go to work / i go to work / i go to work / dilân says – i love you dad / dilân says – but i love mum more / i go to work / four days in a row / 5,6,7,8 / im tired / when i go home i also go to work but i dont say that / centrelink says sophie doesnt work / its a lot of work being a parent, people say / it must be a lot of work / how do you do it? they say, i cant imagine / but i go to work and i work / i come home and i work and i work / on fridays i dont go to work but when my dad asks i say – im at work – because i am, im writing, im working / sometimes i ride to work / sometimes i ride to work with dilân on the back and drop her at childcare / sometimes i run beside her as she rides / i walk to work / i drive to work / i catch the tram to work / i get dropped off at work / im yet to work from home, my industry doesnt allow it / sometimes i say to people that i go to work to rest, work begins when i get home / i say things like – i better go to work – im running late for work – i cant be bothered going to work today – sorry ive gotta go to work – i just knocked off work / my payslip says i worked 30 hours this week / some people work 60 hours a week but im not impressed / sophie works 168 hours a week / my grandma, who they say never worked, said to me – work ender work a lot work hard you must work / my grandma worked at home and from home / i call my grandpa from work on a sunday and tell him im on lunch break and he is impressed – oooow he says very good / my grandpa worked until he did his back / my mum went back to work when i was 1 / my mum still works / the working class works / the middle class middles / i go to work / the dishwasher works / this pen works / the cars getting fixed / this deodorant really works / does the ant work?

/ does the mushroom get time in lieu? / does this swimming pool ever relax? / this worker, it is said, works for the boss / works for the man / the nuclear family doesnt work / the father works / the mother labours / the child plays / the child gets schooled / the child is prepared for work / a guy i worked with said he needed 2 million bucks to retire / a work death balance / some people say they love their work / some people hate their life / i go to work / this must be a great place to work they say to me at work / we came to australia as workers / to work / australia is good for work, turkey is good to live, people say / australia might be a workers paradise / maybe this is a wonderland where each human received the basics of life, food shelter healthcare culture community / when i lived in turkey my music teacher said that hed only once been to another country, bulgaria when it was communist – how was it? i asked – fantastic he said people were out on the streets and in the bars drinking talking and singing every night

## In Real Life

first thing in the morning she barrels in
daaaaad lets play frida kahlo fell off the bus
ok let me wake up a little
daaaaad get up
i get up
dilân lies on the couch
shes frida now
i pull a blanket over her
shes recuperating
sad face fluttering eyes
im making coffee shes
writhing in pain
yesterday i fell off the bus she says no today i fell off the
bus i just fell off the bus
ooooooo are you ok?
nooo i need to rest we
hit the tram and i fell off the bus
my leg is broken
my back hurts
i was covered in gold
my sister helped me christina
she helped me
i take frida milk and drawing materials
place them beside her bed
simulate a knock at the door
someones at the door i call out
everyone can come to visit me she says but

they have to be quiet
and she falls asleep
i open the door and wave everyone in
hi everyone come through but please be quiet dilân
i mean fridas
recovering
she fell off the bus
i sit the visitors down with careful gestures
frida writhes a bit more
frida sits up now
hiiiy she strains
this morning i fell off the bus
it was very loud
it was very crazy
everyone was crying
but im getting better now
frida gets up slowly now
heroic / winces / hobbles / smiles
now shes walking freely its a miracle
ooohh she falls over
i pick her up and
carry her back to bed
weve been playing frida kahlo fell off the bus every morning
for two months
ever since we isolated
and she asked about the frida retablo on her wall
began to embody frida as recovery and resistance icon
we read the story over and over
polio at 6
one leg thinner than the other

fell off the bus at 18
long skirts
mirror above her bed
painting as recovery
art / therapy / communism / diego / feminism / chronic pain /
mexico / eyebrow / blue house / miscarriages / america / lovers /
queer / trotsky / art / death / fame
i brought the retablo back from mexico i say
i visited her house you know
in real life? she asks
yeeeeah ten years ago / the blue house
did you meet her dad?
no shes dead but i went into her house
is she in mexico heaven?
yeah she is
can i send her a drawing?
of course you can
we have stopped playing frida fell off the bus
now we play secret garden
sometimes frida is a special guest
colin is crying in bed
colin is rescued by mary
mary wheels colin to the garden
they garden
the garden comes to life
bright colours like fridas garden
colin starts to walk again
colin is healed
now we stop playing secret garden
now we play jethro and emmett

two brothers from child care
one is six the other is three
they are plumbers
and we fix pipes under the dinner table

## Funk N Wagnalls

our neighbours are both mathematicians
they have two girls at school
the younger girl is about 10
walks around churning a rubiks cube
can solve it pretty quick
her dad is proud but says
shes just using a brute force algorithm
soon shell be ready for a more sophisticated one
itll be much faster
damn i think
maybe all i have is brute force
i remember hitting that wall in maths
maybe later than most
but hitting it hard still
and in all these other fields of life too
at least i read a lot as a kid
not so much a canon
but anything with words on it
newspapers / car magazines / womans day / atlases / yellow pages
white pages
books on the deep sea
books on dinosaurs
stats on the back of basketball cards
i didnt see my parents reading books
but they fed them to me
it was the first half of the 90s
i was in primary school

learnt that the most important
tools were maths skills
general knowledge
and noticing things
in other words
problem solving
memory
and paying attention
this is a migrants world
wed go over to my grandparents house
and id check my babaannes lotto ticket
wed play cards
my dede would write me up
arithmetic problems
and id ask him questions about the world
like whats the history of pakistan?
hed have an answer
the world was enormous i realised
and my world was small
hed stay up every night
reading the turkish encyclopedias
hed brought over when they migrated
my mum was onto it
and started buying me encyclopedias too
from the no frills supermarket at westfield
airport west
when you spent a certain amount
they were 2 bucks each
we collected the set
and id read them

like my dede did
dipping in anywhere
just to absorb it
but who knows where it went
what this training allowed
my mums mum / my anneanne
got her own set
tho she cant read english well
i still see them thirty years on
high up on her living room shelf
1111111111111111111111
every single one is A–American Elk
and American Elk says
–SEE, WAPITI

## Are You Ready Poem

1911 / governor of istanbul orders stray dogs to be rounded up and exiled to the island of sivriada / hunger and thirst / they eat one another / 80,000 dogs perish / some drown at sea trying to escape / a severe earthquake follows / a punishment from god / the island is now aka hayırsızada / the inauspicious island / 2022 / now the accountant tells me hes reading moby dick / tells me i should try to increase my income this year / tells me it hasnt quite grabbed him yet but his son loves it / tells me at this stage a bank wouldnt give us a loan to buy a house in / say / reservoir / my father tells me to become a teacher / on smith street i bump into a friend / 31 / a photographer / works at coles / rainbow lanyard / hes trying to become a firefighter now so that he can become an artist / four days on four days off / 80k and 9wks holiday / time to read on the clock and play ping pong / sounds good to me sounds too good to me / why dont we become poets to become poets / why dont we show the way / my father tells me to become a teacher / my friend the late great poet was penniless at 40 / told me she shouldve done law like kafka and written on the side / died with a million under her pillow at 69 after quitting poems for a while and giving her body to the institution / left everything to a rich friend / he gave up art at 22 / my father tells me to become a teacher / for the second time and the first time in ten years i have a job with annual leave / christmas and new year we go away / i check my payslip and its not there / i tense up / rear up / email payroll / who are lovely / check your payslips / my partner and our friend and i drive to a place called gobarup to look at a property / 100k for 20 hectares / maybe the cheapest land in the state / feels auspicious / a trust for nature covenant / ants everywhere / they come up at you / you cant stand still / the owner suggests we build a wooden platform 8ft high with moats around the uprights to enjoy calm and the nice breeze above the shrubbery / he loves it / his friends wont come here / his wife stays at the gate / he used to work in a bookshop like me / retrained / hasnt gotten around to constructing this platform but it would unlock some potential / a labour of love / bought it from his uncle whod tried to clear it and farm it but the bush is real and the soils hydrophobic / he wants to pass it into good hands / afterwards at the local pub / horses racing on tv / we buy a round / only a few regulars glancing at us / one of them puffs up and charges at me / nose to nose / reckons i might work in the sex industry / points to my tshirt / planet x noosa heads / wants to fuck someone or someone up / i know what to do / ive seen this before / my body tightens / i try to look him in the eye but no good / one goes one way and the other goes another / he sits back down / i want to talk to him now / my father tells me to become a teacher / in the car later my friend / 35 / who is seated behind me / likes that the land is so punk and that split 6 ways we could get it for 15k each / which we dont have yet / tells me that after her phd she might have to stop making art in order to afford to live / but how do we live if we dont make art / can you farm ants / art everywhere / my grandpa dies / my father gives the imam money / the imam politely asks about our family / my dad says hesagoodboy but no direction / a writer / the imam says poets write the world into being / are remembered forever / my father considers this / wonders if im a poet / the technician gels my partners belly / our 3 year old sits on my lap / sees her sibling 27.6mm long / 9wks & 4d in utero / heart172bpm / the technician says very good / i have six months until writing will have to take a bigger backseat / we will have to get a bigger car instead of an ~~art~~ ant colony / maybe the imams should run australia / maybe we could become imams / just for one day / maybe the imams could become artists / my father really wants me to get a steady wage / my mum is less prescriptive / my mum backs me / you say of course she does / i dont want to beg / maybe we could do this together / reader / are you ready / we can be workers together / why should art and writing be solo / lets start an artists and writers league / seize our own means / pool all money / guarantee an income and a place to live / no more platforms / we be the ants now / no more sole trading freelancing grants prizes tenders agents gallerists commercial jobs casual jobs side jobs shit jobs steve jobs / watch the ants / work in league / a common project / get capitalism out of our bones / refuse / this world is a kind of woeful organised stealing / can we make an alternative / dream the world anew / start with our own material conditions / lead by this example / make something dangerous / an artists and writers league / something beyond an ethical art / a radical art / which is radical life / black mountain and co-ops and unions and aris and zines and a koala logo / art as the risk of creating the new / a public will support us / if we support one another / if we can ban plastic bags and cfcs / we can abandon abns and phds / it would be thrilling / when the average artist earns ____ / when housing costs ____ / why not / how to make a dignified life / lets pool money so we all get wet / into the sea like stray dogs

**Erotics Of Bookselling**

hello were the bookshop where we always say yes
how can i help you?
ender speaking
how can i help?
ender
e n d e r
ender
no no turkish
istanbul ankara baklava
so how can i help you?
let me look it up
bear with me
next please!
can i help you?
would you like a paper bag?
tap on the left
have a good day
have a nice day
have a great day
come with me and lets see if we can find it
we should have it
let me ask my colleague
i havent read it but ive heard good things about it
youll love this
this is great
shes great
i havent read this but ive read her other stuff

i didnt like the last one as much
its been selling like hotcakes
people cant get enough of her
good question
let me look it up on our system
weve got one in stock
i can transfer it
i can get one from the supplier
i can order one in
about two days
about a week
about two weeks
let me calculate it
32.99 39.99 59.99 69.99
nice to meet you
pleased to meet you
good to see you
great to see you
good to hear from you
nice to hear from you
nice shirt
i like your haircut
thanks for that
sorry about that
do you play indoor soccer?
no worries
no stress
no problem at all
nothing to worry about
thats my job

thank you

take care

cheers

ok bye now bye bye

no / thank you

no no / thank you / thanks for coming in

im sorry about that

thanks for your patience

theres not much i can do im afraid

im so sorry

its out of print

it was published in 1803

and we last had it in 1997

if you want to try amazon you know where i stand

good luck

i really dont understand the ins and outs of australia post

its out of my hands really

its a big issue no doubt

its systemic

supply chain

covid cargo ships

the exchange rate

the suez canal the bloody ship didnt run aground it got wedged

john howards gst

american express

we can wrap it for a small donation to our foundation

beautiful day out there

cold out there

rainy out there

wealthy out there

yeah its a good job<br>
   its fine<br>
      its a market economy<br>
ooo la la<br>
            nice stack youve got there<br>
i dont mind<br>
   its no big deal<br>
      dont worry<br>
         dont mention it<br>
            look im sorry<br>
               my bad<br>
                  its a shame<br>
               it is what it is<br>
            its been ages hasnt it?<br>
         its been a while<br>
                  its been too long<br>
            its been a pleasure<br>
yeah yeah yeah yeah yeah yeah yeah yeah yeah yeah yeah yeah<br>
   yes yes yes<br>
      yes we can<br>
         the customer is always / the customer<br>
   ok bye bye bye bye thank you baa-bye bye bye<br>
love you ok bye thank you thank you yeah i will yeah say hi<br>
   too bye bye now see you later bye love you mwah<br>
        can you say hi to everyone for me?<br>
    say hello<br>
  send my regards<br>
send my love<br>
  say hi<br>
    hit me up

text me
call me anything
drop in
ill swing by
see you soon
love u
take care
ciao
bye

## Hot Water

three cups of water on the counter and
one of them is hot
sophies telling me a story
i pick one cup up
the right one
at the wrong moment
oouph
gush it out over the floor
burnt tongue sore for days
seems like a dream now
remembering a visit to my friend seçkin
in istanbul
bare cold flat / rugs
no running hot water
he was still asleep when i got there
and kept knocking
he let me in
stoked the fire
filled the kettle
propped it onto the stove
we call it a billy i said
he liked that / bili
told me hed decided to learn to play
the ney
and his teacher had said
dont blow into it! just hold it
for six months

carry it around
get to know the instrument
get the instrument to know you
he poured the boiling water into a bucket
half filled with cold
and said gimme a moment
to bathe
and i said tabii
and thought about all the time spent staring
at blank pages or blank screens or blank walls and how this blankness
this time
this waiting relates to
a watched pot never boils
and to poetry
and im told we see ten thousand ads a day
and in spanish advertencia means warning
and sophie says to me
the hot water bottle has an advertencia
do not use boiling water
so what kind of water do you use?
in istanbul our bathroom basin
had two faucets one for cold one for hot
and i wondered how i could just wash my
hands with warm water without plugging it
and now im thinking of
muhsin kut who lived in bakırköy istanbul
and wanted to be an architect
but his family vetoed study abroad
so he learnt to paint
and later in 1969 at 31 he arrives in sydney

and locals say to him
you have no choice
youll make as much money as your willingness
to do the dirtiest most tiring work and
so muhsin walks into a balmain soap factory
and they say
youre a painter!?
what are you doing here?
how are you gonna do this job?
and to that muhsin replies
leave that to me
cos its like this
im selling you my time
youre the boss
you tell me what to do and i do it
you pay me
and theres no problem…
the boss likes this and says
you sound like the ideal worker!
the job is yours!
now watch how oil melts under hot water!
and hands him a hose
so muhsin kut works there for six years
goes back to turkey for five where he
works as a cartoonist for a newspaper
returns to sydney and regains his old job
for another six
twelve years in a balmain soap factory
paints when he can
saves money

visits turkey every two years to put on a show and
when he secures aussie citizenship in 1986
he goes back to bakırköy
secured so he can
paint
for good and
in 1988 the soap factory closes
and in 2013, 14, 15, 16, 17 & 2023
while wandering the istanbul modern
his painting *Tünelde Müzik Dükkânı* hangs before me
the work of a man unafraid of
and unfazed by hard labour
and the reason im drawn to it is
his bio mentions his stints in australia
and i see it
an artist propelled to the antipodes
running away / caught up
trying to be good
trying to satisfy desire
trying to not go mad
trying to keep it simple
worker artist son bird
and remember when you run a bath dont test the temperature
with your hand but with your elbow
and when like this morning your car windscreen
is frosted up pour cold water
not hot
across the glass
like i do from my water bottle
the kids in their seats

i turn on the engine
blast the hot air / wipers going / fingerless gloves
off to school
i love you
and i love that you rawdog it 80% of the time
i say to sophie
like 80% is the sweet spot for me
rawdog as in
TO PERFORM ANY ACT RECKLESSLY
OR WITHOUT PREPARATION. A MEASURE OF RISK TAKING.
and we reformulate rawdogging at length
as a willingness to take on any situation
with courage and style like
walking in the rain
jumping into a river
riding a bike anywhere anytime
taking bush wees
sitting on the floor
eating nuts out of your pocket
telling the truth
and in general using and cultivating the ability to improvise
and be mercurial
we decide that
two of our friends are 95% rawdog
which brings you to the brink
but makes you irresistible to us
so much wild energy
so maximal with love
this is the human animal
this is the human heart

and this is the human brain which consists of 86 billion neurons
and has a capacity of 37 PETAFLOPS
or 37 quadrillion floating-point operations a second
which is to say that
one flop is
a calculation
and the human brain is capable of a lot of calculations
very fast
while using the energy it takes to glow a small lightbulb
and a supercomputer
needs 6 million small lightbulbs of energy to reach 1.19 PETAFLOPS
but in order to emulate the brain processes in-full
a supercomputer requires 2400 times more computing power
than the brain
or 88,000 PETAFLOPS
taking 528 billion lightbulbs worth of energy
which is all to say
dont leave the world to the oligarchs and their goons
eat well / ride your bike / watch the starry night
and be ready
rawdog it 55–95% of the time
in your skull is the most powerful thing in the known universe
and turning on the hot water for showers it takes
about 19 seconds to warm up
and in that time i stand to the side and begin
brushing my teeth yet when im at my best
i catch the cold water with
a bucket for toilet flushes or the garden
yes cold showers
steel the mind and energy but

the chinese doctor doesnt recommend it
and nor do my grandparents
although i swim in the sea at any time
cos thats a rush
and im a pisces
with an affinity for stingrays and when
samantha offers me a chinese date and says
cut it up and
steep it in hot water for fifteen minutes
i do
cos herbs and wholefoods and remedies
are all around us
and sometimes i just eat parsley rawdog
cos its good for you
and around the time swimming became
acceptable and even cool
during the early days of turkeys republic
my babaanne
would dive off the pier in bakırköy
and come up with a fistful of sand
to whistles and applause
they called her deniz kızı / the mermaid
and my dede fell in love with her for it but
she damaged her ears for life
surgeries hearing aids
a fella called doctor george gray
she claimed
saved her hearing / just 40% in one ear
and her babaanne saved
her leg cos as a child

she got frostbite walking to school through the snow
potions elixirs and a spoon of fish oil everyday
for six months fixed her and
now i take fish oil everyday too cos
sport and manual labour messed up my knees
you werent built for heavy work
shed say to me
after i got a hernia working in a warehouse
and ten years later she reminded me of it when i was in istanbul
on scholarship money watching
porters work from the window of my studio
ben hammal olmak istemiyorum babaanne dedin
and when my friend isadora and i shake hands
she jousts
never worked a day in his life!
and i say
hey come on! thats not true! ive got sensitive skin!
i got 37 PETAFLOPS up here!
and when i wash the dishes
i use gloves
but isadoras hands are rough and strong
i admire her
dirt under nails from the garden
i had once developed callouses
but only from doing chin-ups
there are some things i cant emulate
and when i worked at a restaurant
we stuck masking tape over generic pump soap
and wrote aesob over it
and laughed so hard

cos thats fancy
and the bourgeoisie wants to watch us strive for that p
now looking at my hands front and back
not like my dedes
the mechanic
but as a kid i thought one day they would be
we changed the oil on his car
rotated the tyres
did some gardening
and washed our hands with this coarse
powdered soap he kept in his garage cupboard
and later in the nursing home
he slowed right down
couldnt walk but still had that
crushing handshake
its hard to get my kids to wash their hands
especially in winter
waiting for the water to warm
and now theyre eating
at isadoras house
and im blowing over ezgis pasta to cool it down
and now curly wants me to blow on his too
and ursula wants me to blow on hers too
and i feel good cos im helping
and im delighting them
and what else is there to life
than helping and delighting one another…
just ask nile rodgers from the band chic
he wrote le freak
*i started out as a peacenik hippy and from that i got more and*

*more politicised, more and more radical, finally one day the national guard beats you up and you say, wait a minute i didnt do anything...*
so he joined the black panther party and later said *being a panther was making breakfast, fixing people's houses and washing the streets. that's what we really did.*
and that sounds very decent i think
i think thats what we should do!
after seventeen years here / half his life / today my friend
moved back to lebanon with his wife and two kids
and im happy for him
reunited with his dad and sister and people and land
but sad cos we lose him and also cos we / my family / never did the same
hes left behind his 1964 mercedes benz
we took it for one last ride
solid and smooth as
i know poetry when i see it
when i hear it
when i feel it
its still rock solid but you gotta treat the rust he said
keep it dry
every few months i receive a message
from a different friend / usually a kiwi / after their citizenship ceremony
new australians are shown a big-screen montage of model migrants
and one of the photos is of me smiling / what a lad!
but i was never naturalised
i was born here
the local council took some promo shots for a gig
i played six years ago
and now i star in ceremonies and pamphlets and

was mr.november in the merri-bek calendar...
at the new northcote pool
in the communal showers
you can adjust the water to make it really hot
in an instant
and this is the best part of
the pool visit
not cos its better than the swim
or the water slide or lying on the grass but cos
its the culmination of those layers
its the climax of that poem
and the poem keeps going
all the way home... you know
my mum was born in eymir köyü near ankara 1960
a village of 1174 people at a height of 764m
without electricity
without running water
without sewerage pipes
but with something we now miss
now that i follow the village on instagram / feel connected
and when dilân was a baby i would stay up late
most nights pre-rinsing her nappies in hot water
at the laundry sink
the jet displacing the shit
the steam coming up hard into my face
we maintained our commitment to
reusable nappies for three years
until i gave up those nights at the sink
for as long as i can remember my
anneanne has drunk ılık su / warm water

and thats eastern medicine
and thats me now boiling the kettle for coffee tea
and sometimes just hot water
yeah you say im getting soft early
trending esoteric
but melbourne winters bite
and most of us have been cut off
from folk knowledge / resold it as self-care
and parade our ignorance
confuse bravado for rationality
so stay warm
wear an undershirt
reach for the thermos
wear slippers in the house
watch out for draughts
and never go out with wet hair!
now im riding down nicholson street
on my way home from work
and three friends are singing linger
by the cranberries / why?
a man walks out of an asian grocer
ciggie dangling from lip
and throws a bowl of steaming water across the road
without looking
sorry! he mumbles
no worries! i yell
and it takes me back 31 years to september 12th 1993
eight years old
in front of the tv on a sunday afternoon watching car racing
the sandown 500

v8 holdens and fords chugging around a track
my dede worked at holden
and then he worked at ford
like many turks
we had a ford
and during the race i delight when
one holden leaks oil onto another holden trailing it
dirtying the windscreen and as
the car roars down the straight / 200k an hour
a crew member leans over the barricade and throws
a bucket of soapy water across the windscreen and
at that speed it shatters
but the glass we learn is special / stays intact / the driver finishes
the lap / pulls into the pits
they rip the windscreen out
and the back one too
the car keeps racing
gets a penalty
for the water splash
and now accruing immense drag
goes slower and slower and doesnt finish the race
and to be in hot water
is to get into a difficult situation
in which you are in danger of being criticised
or punished
and i feel like im always
getting into hot water
getting into a bath
and to take a bath
is to suffer a defeat / often financial

and as the economy was tanking
during the lockdowns and i was home on jobkeeper
i would take dilân for a walk to
northcote high school every morning
and after rain worms would wriggle
off the oval and onto the netball court
to either get picked off by birds
or cook as the court dried up
wormies! wormies! shed shout
as we attempted to repatriate them
back to the oval
but did they want to return?
worms have brains
they can feel but they cant think
cant process emotions
cant vote
in theory the human brain has infinite memory
and all memory is long-term
but the architecture of the human mind
and the image of thought
from what i sense
is...
and the poem is a psychic luna park of associations
that just come when the soils ready
and while i tell sophie a story about a character
named domenic
she looks back at me and says
gromenic? thats an unusual name
and i yell its not gromenic!
its domenic!

and we laugh for days
and i can! believe her mind went there
didnt reject that possibility
cos thats the tendency to be open-minded
which i adore
lets remember our first date
a saturday morning she rode her bike to my place
and i was still in the shower / typical
we had planned to go to
the melbourne general cemetery
to get succulents for her pots
but first to a café nearby
she had a latte and
i ordered a breakfast of champions
i was giddy i think barely managing to stay cool
there she was in front of me / my god!
getting ready for her market stall
i told her the elvis shrine was a grotto
that had every kind of succulent
she would ever need
i think she was amused enough
my housemate and her boyfriend were meant
to come with us
but dipped out / with a nod
they say with romance
you dont know what youre getting into
i was going all in
i just wanted to hang out / real bad!
cos she was always making things
playing rather than scheming

and i wanted to play with her too
and a few weeks later
she stood up on it and said
lets jump on your bed!
and broke a slat
but i didnt care...
i want to mention that
muhsin kut didnt come to australia alone
he came with his partner
but i dont know her name
she worked in the soap factory for 18 months
also worked in a nursing home
and as a couple they sold kebabs at markets together too
and when they got back to türkiye
he had a show at the amerikan kültür merkezi
and made 3000 liras and
spent 1800 in one drop at a bookshop
to set up his library and
i wonder if she supported that splurge
but you know who had a good library too?
the last caliph of the ottoman empire
abdülmecid II
one of the most important painters in late ottoman art
his self-portrait hangs in the istanbul modern right
near muhsin kuts painting
and before he was sent into exile
he wrote to atatürk asking for a larger allowance
and the new leader replied
*your office, the caliphate, is nothing more than a historic relic.*
*it has no justification for existence. it is a piece of impertinence*

*that you should dare write to any of my secretaries!*
soon abdülmecid II was collecting butterflies
in exile
his books left behind
he boarded the orient express at 5am on the morning of
the abolition of the ottoman caliphate
goodbye
and my friend tom who likes car racing
says youve gotta have mechanical sympathy
which means to care for the machine
dont jump curbs
get serviced
and make sure
to let the engine warm up
on a cold morning

## Airport

my grandparents or uncles and aunties and cousins are returning home from returning home / the rest of the family early morning pilgrims to the airport / waiting for the silver doors to slide open / arrivals board spasming / DELAYED / LANDED / we all live close to the airport / international arrivals hall now / its 615am in the 1990s 2000s / perhaps all these memories have become one / poem / my mums parents have returned home / they say australia is home now / they say this might be their last time back / they like their home here their backyard here / my dede has arrived with new teeth / i am bamboozled / he is a handsome man / he has a new suit too and a tan / my anneanne has a new beret and gold / shes beautiful / my cousins and i have been waiting / playing with trolleys / we will get to school late this morning / we might get hash browns from maccas / an indenture is a legal contract that reflects an agreement between two parties / usually labour servitude / they say you only belong to a country when you bury a loved one in it / we kiss our grandparents quickly / one on each cheek / we try unzipping their luggage for gifts / who got what / i get a rip-off galatasaray top tho my team is fenerbahçe and also a silver chain / we dont make the pilgrimage anymore / but i offer pick-ups and drop-offs all the time / its good to see a friendly face on the other end / back then the aura of travellers / some gold dust that rubbed off onto you / probably more for me / id never been to turkey but i was turkish / our backyard was under a flightpath / look up and imagine / my cousin forgot how to speak english after six months there / my cousins with grandparents there / i had great-grandparents there i never met / my parents didnt take me back / my parents couldnt look back / my mum said too painful / my dad said you gotta move on / when home alone mum listened to turkish music / australia told us no dont go back / work / a debt / australia a spell / australia using up the best of us / my mum with a pocket koran in her bag / we were always close to the airport / zeki dede worked at istanbul airport / ali dede worked at ankara airport / thats how they got here / zeki dede worked at essendon airport / my dad worked at tullamarine airport / i did my work experience at the airport / mum took me to roger david and we bought two shirts a tie and pants / wed buy kfc and drive out to the airport to watch the planes land with dad / or take off / an airport a black hole that sucks in all around it / they say direct flights will soon start from melbourne to istanbul / just go to sleep and youre there / youre home / in istanbul they lived near the airport / my dedes dad was buried on its edge / one day they said – were expanding the airport so come dig up your kin / so my dede went and dug up his dad / exhumed his remains / and put him in a new cemetery / almost sixty years later / my dede dies / is buried at fawkner cemetery under a flight path / he dies while i am living in istanbul / i go to the cemetery and find his mum and dad and sit with them / merhaba i say aloud ben senin büyük torununum / ŏglun zeki benim dedemdir / çok uzaklarda / topraklara verildi / başımız sağ olsun / allah rahmet eylesin

## Get Your Overalls On

ww2 turkey trying to stay out of it / neutral / afterwards america wants to bring democracy / puts pressure / welcome to nato! / cold war / military coup / hang the prime minister / reform / workers first allowed to unionise in 1961 / the left getting stronger / growing class consciousness / conditions ripening for revolution / america no like this / so funding the right wing / ultranationalists and clerics / operation gladio / counter-guerilla / look it up / escalation of political violence / assassinations / cia / may day massacre / amongst it all leftist artists prominent / musicians singing about social issues about politics in a direct way / a long tradition in folk music now crossing into rock and pop / not just singing of naive love but of social conditions / of oppression / of class / the giant presence cem karaca / iconic singer / the resonator / singing tamirci çırağı / 1975 / listen to this song / deep booming voice / the music swells and slows / rock / full of a drama of the street / a glamourous woman / brings her car to mechanic / an apprentice swoons / overnight he thinks of a novel hed read / the same situation / beauty falls for a worker / next morning brushing his hair / waits / asks his boss if he can go without wearing his dirty overalls today / she walks in / hes agog / trying to be smooth / he opens the car door for her / whos this bum? she snorts / she gets in / stomps the gas pedal / chokes him with fumes / he is crushed / tears bud / boss slaps him on the back and cem karaca sings *unut dedi romanları işçisin sen işçi kal giy dedi tulumları* / forget the novels – you are a worker – stay a worker – get your overalls on / line repeats twelve times to end the song / you are a worker stay a worker ////////////////////////// in billy joels america / reagans america /

1983 / the dream / mtv / an uptown girl will tire of her white bread world / desire a red-blooded downtown man / the lyrics offer no description of a scene / just a vague scenario / rich girl poor boy / the film clip does the lifting / unlike the social realism of tamirci çırağı this song ends neither in consummation or rejection but pure fantasy / in the film clip joels real-life future-wife christie brinkley arrives at the mechanics in a chaffeur-driven rolls royce / shes easily charmed by joel and his crew / virility of the lower classes / joel wrote the song / inspired by frankie vallis song rag doll about a poor girl rich boy / so i just flipped it around he said / things move quickly in the three-minute clip / brinkleys a supermodel / shes on a billboard ad above the workshop / her poster inside joels locker / her car arrives / joel and his crew approach the car / encircle it like wolves / joel isnt seen cleaning it the others are / extreme vitality / brinkley smiles / lowers her window / steps out of the car / joel and his crew pursue her / she walks without a clear purpose / shes coy / no longer smiling / her black chaffeur is unimpressed by the white boys / the song hits the bridge / it gets to her / suddenly shes linedancing with joel and his crew along with two bikers and two young black guys / logic is broken / or this is a dream / this is ideology / this is art? / joel and brinkley ride off on a motorcycle / you know the song / 50s doo-wop / appropriated / post-war nostalgia / class is eclipsed by race / this might be the fantasy / that in america white people can overcome class but for black people not so easy / black characters remain on the periphery / remember in real life joel does get the girl / he wrote the song for his girlfriend elle macpherson / confidence / man / then he marries brinkley / but he is the pop star not the worker / or if we look closer into the clip we see / his uniform is slightly different / hes wearing a shirt / the others are wearing overalls / we see the others working on the tools but never him / joel the boss / the piano man / a good student apparently / missed a high school exam / said – *to hell with it. if i'm not going to columbia university, i'm going to columbia records, and you don't need a high school diploma over there* ////////////////// my dede was a plane mechanic / thats how my dads family got to australia / on a plane / he got a job at essendon airport / got a second job at the holden plant / left the jobs to run a petrol station with my dad / dede fixed the cars / dad pumped the fuel / along with some turkish boys / one became crazy john mobile phone baron / hero of the turkish diaspora / rock hard proof of upward mobility / australias a good country / my mum was learning to drive at the kmart car park across the road / shed drive in for fuel / maybe he waved the younger boys away / grabbed the bowser himself / early 80s / can you imagine / billy knew something / they got married / meanwhile 1980 fascist coup d'état in türkiye / america pushed the button / my mums uncle a leader in the teachers union thrown in jail along with thousands of comrades / karaca in exile in west germany / a warrant out for his arrest / singing in german on tv / repression and depression in türkiye / simple life in australia / in the colony / im born / mum gets a government job / a typist an assistant / works her way up / still there / dad becomes a worker again / dede becomes a worker again / dad starts working for himself / no employees just him / they took me out of public school / into private school / first to graduate uni in my family / tried for government jobs / tried for grad programs / rejected / confused / my dad loves the frankie valli musical jersey boys / he and mum have seen it six times / i start writing / work moving furniture / hospo / call centre / warehousing / labourer / work in maintenance / work as a caretaker of a school / join the union / work in a bookshop now / believe in the poetics / being against capital means being for life / arts defunding / welfare state crumbling / family as safety net / the dead labour of my family secures me / and my kids / my partner / video of me first year of school 1990 / all the kids asked by our teacher / what do you want to be when you grow up? / im pretty shy / im pretty sweet / i want to be a mechanic when i grow up / but dede says to me later – study ender study... you need education ///////////////////////// *Gönlüme bir ateş düştü yanar ha yanar yanar / Ümit gönlümün ekmeği umar ha umar umar*

## Kadiköy

they say this is a migrant nation
others say settler colony
for some
we can go back to where we came from
to see with our own eyes!
so we go back to türkiye
we take our kids
my first time i was 23
dilân and ezgi / five & one now
together we eat warm bread
a huge ship / empty / riding high
glides through the bosphorus
ukranya! says someone in the teagarden
grain corridor! i hear on the news
a heatwave / our beaded foreheads
dilân runs through sprinklers
a kids park in the full sun
playgrounds without tanbark
but with hot sand
we lived here once
sophie and i / six & seven years ago
back at our old grocer
the deli guy remembers us / seems worn down
maybe the heat i think
hes lost his / french word
the next day he says to me

brother
& takes a deep breath
stress is the killer...
he works seven days
how much can a person carry
my dad retired
dodged a heart attack by days
his doctor said youve won the lottery!
a stent a spring
his doctor motivates him now
to cut salt so salt
dad says is a silent killer
and desk jobs and loneliness
hes been researching silent killers
they say find what you love and let it kill you
and maybe its harder to find in some places
every few days here in türkiye they announce
a terrorist has been neutralised
a soldier has been martyred
in australia we dont announce such things
but across the bosphorus and up the road in 2017
ai weiwei said to us
that anyone telling the truth about their country
is already well on their way to jail
he said his father entered jail an artist
and came out a poet
cos jail took away everything but poetry
and the conceit of australia
is that all bad things happen in other places

and im reading a book by
nâzım hikmet
about loving life
about being on the run and in jail
and it knocks me out
the torture the suffering and the love we
are deprived of by living in a mad world
validating again the fear of this state
that was hung around my neck
they say to me no human rights in turkey
they say theres a dictator
they say to me australia good country
they say australia bin good to us
they say australia also redneck country
they say australia this and australia that
and now i stop thinking of australia
we have rented an apartment for a month
in our old neighbourhood kadıköy
the footpath ripped up at the front door
no one fixes it
the bricks just piled up
cats sit on
cats shit on it
we carry ezgis pram over it
some graffiti on the wall says
my friends are in berlin
and im stuck in this nightmare...
we have two old friends from here now living
somewhere near hamburg

ahmet went to study
and bal waited nine months for her visa
got on the plane the day after it came
they are back in istanbul tomorrow and
i will get their opinion on the matter as
the turkish lira plummets
and we are in a fourth-floor apartment
from the front end we see the street
and from the back balcony a panorama of courtyards
balconies tarps patch up jobs hanging laundry and a building site
we see turkish flags and a mosque
dilân says goodnight world! waves the scene to sleep
the sun dips / last call to prayer means bedtime
i tilt the pedestal fan to flow across the bed
in turkey if you started work before september 8th 1999
you can get your pension
after 20 (women) or 25 (men) years
of work with at least
5000 / 5975 days worked
regardless of age
but the younger generation must work til 58 or 60...
in the mornings dilân and i run down the stairs
to the bakery that makes simit
two kurdish brothers run it
and they love dilân
love her name and her spirit
she holds my hand and watches them work
the dough slides down the chute from the kitchen above
the woodfire oven sunken into the ground

one of the brothers is sweating in the pit
arms wrapped with towels
arranging the dough
on the wooden paddle
the other brother packing the bread and serving us
we buy three simit and they chuck another one in for free
along with some nutella
and a wedge of laughing cow cheese
and i urge her to say
teşekkür ederim and dilân mumbles it
burhan bends down and smiles at her
they say güle güle and we say hoşça kal
walking holding hands along the early morning street
saying merhaba kedi
climbing up the spiral staircase
dilân crawls the last flight
we knock
sophie opens the door
the table is set
chopped cucumbers tomato cheese olives acuka honeycomb
and grape molasses... allahu ekber!
hard for kids here
no grass no beach few trees no merri creek
we cut in half a plastic bottle and fill it with water
for the street cats watching
waiting for them to come and drink it
its school holidays
barely any kids around
make your own fun

at sundown they come out to play on the street
at the playground a kid speaking russian
doesnt want to play with dilân
so we play together instead
a game she invented called celia and struin
the teenage step-sister and dad of her friend neve
i am struin and this wobbly sprung playground motorbike is my
whip im driving from northcote to st.kilda to pick up celia
and bring her home for the weekend
but celia is reluctant to hop on
we stage the tension between a teenager and father
a proto-future that pre-exists here and now that dilân is already
tired of being away from her friends her toys her room after
two weeks but two months still to go
daaaaad can we go home now?
she has started to bite us when things dont go her way
and yesterday she threatened to jump out the window...
sophie and i are scrambling
up late formulating tactics and new plans
how can we give her what she needs
when this city we love isnt
and the deli guy says to me
you look great
dont say that i say
his coworker in fruit&veg says
what are you doing here? dont even think about moving back here
why?
rezil! he says the situation is very bad / enflasyon savaş siyaset
grain ship after grain ship

slip into the bosphorus
are you alive? gabe texts
to the fingertips i reply
its true
im reminded here that i am alive
some frisson then too much
hitting limits
even on holiday
the heat the crowds the risky footpaths
the figs the grapes the honey the hum
the fresh bread the brewing tea the sticky molasses
the cat shit the smog the singing and dancing in the streets
the young boys headphones in diving into dumpsters
for plastics and cardboard to cash in
hey theres the blue mosque in the distance
the hagia sofia and topkapı palace
by far the highest consumers of bread in the world
16 million getting bread / the conquest of bread
but where are the kids on the streets
why are the seagulls enormous
the dogs so sleepy
two kids here and a wad of cash in my pocket i like
this breeze this view the flap of the umbrella
lets keep it simple
we take a walk dilân and me
to visit my old music teacher
he buys her an ice cream
he has five sons
but always wanted a daughter

we sing dilo dilo yaylalar
and say goodbye
dilân points out an old sculpted door handle made of metal
and says that looks like tracey
her favourite button and i say
youre so perceptive
shall i come back with you to austria?
the fruit&veg guy says while his teenage son weighs
bags of cucumbers and tomatoes
ill work ill do any job for $1500 amerikan dolar!
thats below the minimum wage i say
how much is that?
i calculate in my head – $2400US a month
alright im in!
but what about your family?
theyll follow
what are your skills?
im a farmer i know animals and plants
are you fit and strong?
he laughs / flexes / i feel his bicep
how old? 36
hes younger than me im rocked i guess he works seven days
a bit old but its possible i say
oh yeah?
my grandparents migrated in their late thirties early forties
and have all lived into old age
but you know its australia not austria right?
arent they the same?
we are down south below endonizya… youve left it a bit late

to be honest cos australia wants your best years!
it can have it! im through with this place
but this is your country! what do *you* think? i turn to ask his son
who smiles like he thinks he should
now dilân is singing from the balcony
from english it turns to her creole
plip stop cring crang
a lito windowanda ching ching
a lito windowanda ching ching
fing fing badiddy bing fig
badiddy fig fig
annady diddo
annady doolah
dadday doolah
ganady doodah
bip bip bip birol
beedee babi bee
carry p carry me
dat sit...
i like haydar dilân says
is that cos he bought you an ice cream?
nooooh
we did sing together i guess / i like him too
we are happy improvising as istanbul demands
we have kids now and our reactors risk meltdown
sensory maximums psychic load
we take taxis without child seats
no problem
we hold ezgi in our arms

clasp hands with dilân
bolting and skating through the traffic some drivers work bitter
its a relief when theyre chill
i sit in the front seat and chat
but now along the üsküdar boulevard
a boy runs out in front of our cab and we hit him
sophie screams
the driver steps out shaking
people crowd around the boy
sophie clutches the kids / covers dilâns eyes
i leap into the back seat to hold them
the crowd is angry at the driver
he says sorry and he also protests / the boy just ran out!
the boy sits up stunned but maybe ok
the driver defeated looks at me
im sorry but you must go
we get into another cab this drivers cranky we dont speak to him
but talk dilân through the trauma
answer her questions
bring it up to the surface
try to purge it
ok now lets go get dondurma
dilân likes the blue gelato they call italian caramel
her two front bottom teeth are wobbly...
nâzıms book is titled
yaşamak güzel şey be kardeşim
which the translators have
rendered – life's good, brother
but to me thats misleading even tho it rolls off the tongue

its more accurately
living is a good thing brother
or
it's good to be alive brother
since yaşamak is to live
and life makes it personal and singular
but hikmet is a communist and
its all about the cause / the rev
and whats important is not how hes feeling
but what it means to be alive...
DONDURMA!
another world is possible
thats what travel makes real
we are trying to give these days shape
bakery playground walk frozen2 ice cream
ever since the flight we have gotten into watching frozen2 on
my laptop in the afternoons we skip through the scary bits
dilân holds our hands and ezgi takes her nap
after frozen2 she plays with her buttons
a box of fifty we packed for her as a pocket world
the most important is tracey
a pale-pink plastic button with cutaways and floral elements
she spreads them across the table and they become
characters in an elaborate drama
SİMİTÇİ! ATEŞ GİBİ!
a man carrying a twelve-storey tray of simit on his head
calls out
SİMİT!
we push the window open
SİMİİİİİTÇİİİİİİİ! we yell

he looks up without moving his head / spots us
we lower the cane basket
with our lira in it
iki tane lütfen / kolay gelsin!
dilân peers down enchanted
the simitçi places his tray onto the bonnet of a parked car
stuffs two simits into a paper bag
unravels the wad of cash
from his pocket to give us change
dilân hauls the rope up and i take up the slack for insurance...
sophie is a coeliac and this is another tragedy / beer oats croissants
missing out on simit with us cuts deep
later that night shes asleep and im reading nâzım
he is still lauded and remembered as an enemy of the rich
and a friend of the poor
his agony his idealism his humour
hits me hard
one of nâzıms jailers says...
*if we applied the law to everyone we'd be in a fine mess*
naasicaa is coming to visit soon
flying in from athens
she loves poetry
lets read poems to one another i think to myself
lets recite poems to one another by candlelight
lets ask what nâzım wonders when
his comrade says to him
*tomorrow, or the day after, we'll return to our country...*
*and we'll meet with hardships, we'll end up in prison, and*
*if in my old age i get used to beds with springs, prison benches*
*will be too hard on me...*

and i become aware of the courage and humility it
takes to return to your country
cos australia mythologises
building a new life in the colony
but what about ditching that and turning back
when youve grown used to it
and we ask ahmet and bal
hows germany?
and ahmet says
i was afraid to call the plumber
when the toilet broke

## On The Peoples Beach

its a public holiday
101 years after the victory
in a war of independence
today the ferry is free
but somehow we pay anyway
the turnstile beeps
the ferry arcs onto truck tyres
we pour on
tipping the ship
sun mangling us this early
as i rub sunscreen onto her
dilân not yet five says
fucken hot
and i say ohhhh yeah
trying to chill
moving it along
hey lets go get cheese toasties and tea
we return
the cheese stretchy the tea double cupped
a woman with rotting teeth smiles at ezgi
asks for a hug / sophie hands her over
people like to smile at ezgi
now everyone wants a hug
diligent and ferocious
dilân brushes her teeth tonight
but on the island now
an electric bus

takes us to the peoples beach
pebbles jellyfish and a hundred lira for a beach chair
we like it here all considered
our friends just flew in from berlin
its perfect isadora says
looking out over the sea of marmara
and i say yeah it is and it isnt
we like it and youre here
i love my friends / trying to live it
i feel like im ok at being grateful / at least nowadays
largely because i never saw a future no glory no arc
so its all bonus now life
doing away with the dominance of narrative is release
not despair so let it come
people here say im lucky / 2nd gen
someone from the bus ride
complains to me about the smell on the beach
says shes had enough
shes going to the private beach
maalesef i say
we should probably be grateful on victory day
a lotta people died and
i cant smell anything
obnoxious despite my large nostrils
just seaweed ciggie butts
the juice and blot of sixteen million souls
whatever it is im here for it
teenagers diving in off the jetty
jellyfish that dont sting
SPF50 slick & coconut oil

sophie blows up dilâns floatie
ezgi asleep on her lap
i hand dilân ten lira for a drink
and she bounds up to the canteen
building confidence
slowly hatching out of monolingualisms egg
i dive under
come up with a jelly on my nog
they dont sting but they glow
the canteen is godly in this heat
run by saints
we buy sparkling water / ayran / nescafé / turkish coffee
beer / fried chips
dilân gets an ice cream sandwich
the chip guy leaps off a boat from the mainland with a sack of potatoes
peels chops drops them into the frier now
they call him usta
his daughter dives off the jetty pindrop and now shes
offering us crisps asking us how old we are
shes ten im thirtyeight dilâns five in a week
we sit in our soggy bathers
playing scopa under the hot tin canteen roof
dilân wins
with the most cards coins and scopas
i like the one of coins most
that jester face magnificent like these
chips
weve become friends with the guys that run this place
its our fourth or fifth visit
they know dilâns name and call her prenses

we know their names their ages their provincial homelands their working conditions and call them abi / bro
they call ezgi
fıstık / peanut
unabashed! full of spirit
ezgi looks one way and
a woman hands us half a watermelon like that
people here see and express joy and hope in children
amidst tough times
wildfires as the lira plummets
power corrupts
and theres no rain
yet people tell me the generation coming up is a beauty
and theyre gonna change things
really deep down theres still hope
like really deep
like the istanbul reservoir at 4% which theyre getting
some special machine to reach the water beneath
now that im a dad twice over and hitting middle age
im hope adjacent
theres no hope in me per se
no special machine
and maybe thats a relief
we discuss this on the beach with sophie aaron and isadora as curly sleeps and we paint watercolours… careers!
do you need some more colour?
youve got a booger in your nose!
three artists and a poet
freaks with niche skills
bad at email paperwork taxation

we belong on islands like this
small arid rocky and slow
im meant to be studying again
instagram says procrastination is a trauma response
but ive got so little time for it now
maybe a cure
dilân says dad lets go for a long adventure
and i say were on one
so we swim a bit
i dive off the jetty twice cos she wants me to
a cool dad / trying hard / staying connected
two tuk-tuks take us back around the island
now weve jammed onto this ferry
ezgi in our arms / dilân gazing into blue
fucken hot
isadora strips curly off
sitting on the timber deck in a sea of legs
the swelter and the lime-green rope python
these are the moments the word fond will flag
a taxi driver says were living what others dream of
sweat thirst and azure rippling past
dilân stares at a woman with a fan attached to her phone
she smiles nudges over and aims it on the kids
we say teşekkür ederim
she says rica ederim
its victory day

## Monolingualism Swamp

in the spice bazaar
handed a cup of eucalyptus tea
they slice and box turkish delight for us
gifts for friends along with
pepper grinders
olivewood spoons
and knock-off footy shirts
yes we are in istanbul
turkish arabic english russian
jawed hammered cobbled alleyways
the man with the precise beard says
no sugar just stevia the natural sweetener
he wants me to sniff crystal menthol
bu kristal mentol bunu deneyin
i like it but do i need it?
offered a generous discount we buy
a small jar of it to present to customs
i know what menthol is
its vicks
but this is the spice bazaar
and im in the hands of virtuosos
a polyglot seller selling in every vector
quantum selling
over his shoulder in arabic he sells lokum
to his left he offers sophie a powder called ottoman spice
you can use it in anything!

now hes handing out pomegranate tea with two hands
infinite arabics & englishes
beyond dialects
a little pidgin then some creole
all the senses
we adjust our tongues
living la lingua franca
i was gifted two languages
whattabout me kids?
they say growing up bilingual is good for your brain
if i say gday its cos i feel like im speaking to a racist
in turkish i call you sibling aunty friend older sister
my beloved simit seller remembers me seven years on
hows your mother?
she calls me kardeş
and i call her sibling too
there are no gender pronouns in turkish
but we have other problems
the poet glissant gave up english like both my dedes
gave up the smokes / late in life
how do we imagine other worlds if we only speak commodity
only speak kings english
so turn off ch7 & radio national and just tune into sbs radio cantonese
for an hour and let the rhythm the melody the harmony reach u
a colonic for your brain
even try 3CR talkback a working-class radical radio
i used to marvel at an old friend of mine whod never change his
speak for anyone a country boy from murray bridge SA
cos it didnt come natural to me

dodging snipes and punches
keeping head down
be a gentleman
my dede said
and he showed me the way
impeccable
but someone threatens you?
punch first
now my friends ask
are you fluent?
we spoke turkish at home but english too
had no satellite dish few imported videos
sometimes id listen to sbs turkish with my dede and
after he died i found a piece of cardboard in his toolbox with
the name of the then president
AHMET NECDET SEZER
my turkish is ok
an alter ego sometimes visits
and i get dark and things flow
the mask goes on or comes off im not sure
im bringing some turkish books back to melbourne
i read them to dilân at night sometimes
shes five and has already asked
but do you read turkish books dad?
gotta lead from the front
the past weeks here in türkiye
feeling her monolingual pain
in 2016 i had a little desk here
in an artisans building on the third floor

next door a fitter and turner
trembling walls
he brings me tea
you wanna come to friday prayers?
looking at my world map on the wall he says
turkeys in the centre of the world bro
right in the centre not like austria thats off-centre
australia!
even worse wheres that? in the ass-end!
one day we left work at the same time
walked side by side
he had just bought a pair of timberland boots
and was feeling pumped
his last pair lasted seven years
and were easily worth the two weeks wages
do you make money writing?
not really
why do you write?
its a habit
do you write in turkish?
mostly english
do people read books in austria?
not much
in turkey no one reads
they like pornos you should write pornos then youll make money
you have a point...
now im in a bookshop
on the aegean
a place called datça

a famous poet lived here
yesterday we visited his final glass of wine
half-drunk evaporated stained and sitting in a wall cabinet
six years ago here i bought a leather-bound book
turkey: a political history
written in english by an american academic
i sat outside the shop and began flicking through it
when an old man announced
young man! i taught the author
and i looked up and asked
this book?
indeed! im a retired professor from the university of ankara
he didnt seem to endorse his student
we were speaking turkish but he grew impatient
switched to a commanding sort of english
but i insisted on my turkish
how can you learn without the patience of a teacher?
from his shirt pocket he drew a pen and paper and wrote down his email
promised to send some readings
i emailed him but he was 90 / never replied
now back again in that shop
the bookseller wants to help me
yardımcı olayım
türk edebayatini ariyorum genelde şiir okuyorum ama roman da olur
he shows me turkish books old and new
this time i ignore the english stock
yaşar kemal shouldve won the nobel he reckons not orhan pamuk
but there were political reasons
ince mehmedi okudun mu / have you read memed my hawk?

no
i tell him i work in a bookshop in melbourne
and that we have yaşar kemal and also sabahattin ali
madonna in a fur coat amongst world classics
he tries to sell me the turkish edition
he wants to know about books in australia
do people read?
what are the prices?
yes and no and higher than here i say
when i opened up seven years ago there were six bookshops
in datça he says
now im the only one
his index finger up between us
a customer walks in
i want a novel she says
theres the new elif shafak he says
no ive read that
really? it just came out
how much is it?
185 liras
do you have anything cheaper?
he selects five books for her and blurbs on each
she dismisses them all to pick up an old jeffrey archer
thats 90 liras he says
hay allahım she says
and walks out
he shrugs
they dont want people to read… they want ignorance!
meanwhile ive chosen seven books new and old

he gathers his pencil and tallies them up
thats 475 liras he says
30 bucks
this will set me up
ill read these books in turkish
my daughters will see me
      thumbing the dictionary

## Catafalque At The Consulate

i kiss my daughters goodnight / motor through the city listening to roy orbison / the big O / handbrake / a queue along the footpath spilling out a foyer / i join it / its midweek / black puffy vests and exercise tights / perfume / i am alone tonight / with my diaspora / all the men have short hair / somebody walking by says – just out of interest what are you all lining up for? / democracy mate says the man in front of me / hands in pockets / no smell of sausages or sujuk tonight / the penultimate day of voting / exercising democratic rights / phroaw its getting chilly huh? he says to his partner / yaaah / second round presidential election / her father calls / she speaks turkish / she reassures him baba baba baba / satisfied voters tumble down the steps like newlyweds / turkish a melodious tongue / a confetti in the air here off st.kilda road / i brought a book with me / wont need it / im feeling it / a buzz / is this what some people feel in front of an apple store? / youre meant to say türkiye now not turkey / but we go back and forth / a backsliding democracy / but arent they all? / the vote but no justice / a record turnout / a tyrant an autocrat a dictator a sultan a strongman / albaneses a nice man / albaneses a paesano / albaneses got wog blood / australias been good to us / the song is *shes a mystery girl* / i cant get it out of my head / learnt today bono wrote it / damn / why dont you go back to where you came from / good question / where did you come from? / its a shame whats goin on in turkey at the moment / ahem youre meant to say türkiye now not turkey / global capitalism / western imperialism / its the air you breathe / this is the luckiest country in the world / its aukus its manus its climate collapse its a janus / a painful horizon / we know how to fix it but we arent in power / our oldest daughter is almost five and she knows everything isnt ok / we must find ways to articulate it / this vicious viscous dread / you shouldnt have to be sensitive to understand it / drowning daily like flies in a treacherous and agonising molasses of alienation and exploitation / so that she can combat it artfully and full of good humour / we show the way sing dance yell and pick up rubbish / yes we have medicare tv aircon free delivery warm water but do we have dignity? / its a jungle out there my dad says / just up the road neo-nazis marching every saturday now / the turkish flag flies above the consulate and the croatian one too / turkish people deeply political they have long memories / im turkish but ive been disciplined here / i walk different i talk different / white australians settlers compradors / high school students with clipboards ask me on my lunch break / do you think multiculturalism is a good thing? / it depends / the big O / in the distance the shrine looms above the canopy / they dont like immigrants who play up / turkey a model modern muslim capitalist democ... / turkey turkey what a lovely country! / turkey cappadocia hot air balloons / turkey aegean sea blues / turkey the diggers went there / turkey good food great hospitality donna kebabs! / türkiye its such a shame whats going on there / shame about the earthquake / i was born here / we came here as workers / albaneses a nice man / grew up in the housing commish / you can trust him he knows poverty hes got wog blood / i paid 1500 euros to get my tezkere / complete military service and finally become a dual national / i havent been to dallas victoria since my babaanne died / been going to basfoods for zeytin and beyaz peynir / dallas where our mosque shops people are / the lobby doors swallow a few of us now / we mince forward / two and half hours! someone declares with a whiff of pride / new nikes / a man abandons the queue / will come back tomorrow / a mother daughter both in black are chewing gum / you could be sisters! someone says / they like that / ive spent 632 days in türkiye my entire life / avukat bey naber? someone salutes the man behind me / i hear their hands slap together / just ah doing my duty he says / hes a young lawyer / hes a bridge between communities / an advocate an avukat an avocado / double exile / so close yet so far / are these my people? / in our photo album a picture of me at eight being awarded a trophy / a lectern a red crescent moon flag hanging backdrop / im dressed smart / i trained with the soccer team north coburg but never played a game / my uncle the vice-president / my father wanted me to play tennis instead / i text my mum and dad now / oyumu kullanıyorum / they came to vote yesterday / i played turkish folk songs on the elektro bağlama along with my serbian friend on drums and lebanese friend on guitar to about 30 people at a brunswick street bar last night / ballot boxes will close at 10pm / lotsa young people here / at 32 i became a citizen / my friend says i shouldnt have a vote / my friend might have a point / my friend is an immigrant / my friend and i discuss the syphoning of labour by global capital / gastarbeiter / am i just a piece of cheap labour? / a consumer / historical forces made us leave / i had no choice in the matter / i dream sometimes of returning / of righting wrong / i was born into this / is this wrong? / in türkiye every morning they scramble jets here we scrambles eggs / police choppers over brunswick / violating our airspace / our breakftast vibe / two friends spot one another / carn the pies! blues are in trouble they gonna sack the coach / collingwood beat carlton yesterday / youre not like the other turks / there might be many ways of being turkish / many ways of being turkish in australia / you dont look turkish / *you* dont look turkish / now its 930 and im in the foyer waiting in line for the elevator / eight at a time / two security guards dressed in tight black shirts and pants / a cortege for turkish democracy / my babaanne loved roy orbison mostly for his suffering / he had a tragic life / they say melbourne winters in weatherboard houses builds character / roy orbison wore black / what other tribulations build my character i wonder / i dont wear black am i naive? / i hear a woman say oh my god if that happens again im gonna throw myself off the balcony / clock winding down / the guards lock the automatic doors / one goes upstairs and the other operates the lift / when people leave dont let anyone else in or there will be trouble – they say to us / someone leaves / a democracy loving man in a denim jacket sneaks in and joins the democratic queue / security catches on a moment later / theyre turkish but they say it in english / hey you cant come in! / why not bro? its not ten oclock yet / the door was locked because we hit our limit / what limit? what time even is it bro? / (its 940) / this isnt turkey alright? you cant do that / what does that mean im not goin anywhere bro im here to vote i drove all the way here after work / hey this isnt turkey here this is australia! / what the fuck does that mean anyway? / it means you cant just do whatever you like here / do what? vote? im not goin anywhere bro! / louder and louder / everyone watching / three young women behind me whispering – oh my god its berats brother i bet you that berats brother like brother like brother can you believe it berats brother oh my god so typical always stirring shit up / security backs down / oh well / security flipping between harsh and generous / the denim jacket man will vote / cnut became king of england in 1016 / fuck its good to be around turkish people / canny anxious crazy curious cracked proud gentle generous intense / i miss it / only now in my late 30s do i really in a deep way understand the difference between my people and the anglosphere / always walking into the wrong room / i miss turkey / türkiyeyi özlüyorum / gurbetçi / even saying hello to the grocer makes me feel / good / these folks dont know me tho / maybe no one knows me here / and i dont know anyone / melancholy for what we keep running from / lives the consequence of other maniacs delusions / in 2016 my father returned there for the first time after 49 years / in 2018 my parents and i voted for the first time from here / they stood beside one another at the booth / mum asked a question / dad answered / an official yelled at him – you cant talk in the booth! / dont speak to me like that / others joined in / someone kicked the official / chairs thrown / one security guard / we ran out / got a coffee downstairs / turks are passionate people! / theres always a lot at stake / why cant we relax? / when people say its a shame whats happening in turkey they irritate me / its a shame what is happening here / i step into the elevator / the security guard reaches in and presses 8 / the lawyer is alert and asks me in english can you press the button? / but the door closes and we begin upwards / sorry he says it didnt light up / bir şey değil i say / on level 8 now / have your id cards ready! / those with id or electoral role irregularities are assisted / sometimes the limbs of the state show mercy / the room is packed with observers and officials / i am given a ballot paper a stamp and an envelope / they ask me to leave my wallet phone and book on the table / i step into the booth / the ballot paper has two names two photos / i stamp the candidate i want / the candidate with the better moustache / slide the ballot into the envelope / lick it seal it place it into a clear box jammed with ballots and hand the stamp back to the booth official / the big O playing in my head / a catafalque is a platform or plinth or framework used to support a coffin / two women sit at the table one holds a pen and paper while the other holds my id card / she looks up at me and reads aloud / ender başkan bin dokuz yüz seksen beş baba adı osman timur / beside her the other woman writes it down / my trembling hand signs my name / the way she said my name / she said it right

## A Poem For Two Euro, 8 Kittens And 50,000 Steps

sharks experience infinite regeneration of teeth
until death
today my friend took 8000 steps at work
showed me the number on his phone
his housemate in a desk job
also took 8000
but worked out in the stairwell on break
they are duelling
everyone is trying to get their steps up
to beat one another
to beat the sedentary lifestyle
to beat heart disease i think
am i the only one trying to get my steps down?
i dont count them but
heartbeats
you only get so many
the chinese doctor says
so i try pouring all my beats
all my spirit all my steps into
the jug of revolution
youre not old!
someone older than me says
youd be surprised i reply
the median age in australia
is 38.5 years old
and im 39!
tongue of the unseen dimensions of reality

you do you
a walk along the merri creek
the trickle and slap of time
im on the edge of flow
when neil armstrong plopped onto the moon
he meant to say
one small step for a man
one giant leap for mankind
but he forgot to say 'a'...
when gabe left our place after staying for a year
the impact on dilân and ezgi was
immense
our dear friend our comrade
no longer here
no longer there for a cuddle in the morning
when we wake up
or a jam in the afternoon
singing edinburgh gardens over and over
and when the world is new and right before your eyes
thats confusing that stings
today dilâns tooth fell out at the dinner table
thats her fourth
and itll be replaced soon
maybe you lose childhood friends like you lose baby teeth
they get replaced into another set
but thats it / until you get veneers
we havent truly lost gabe
he will be back
but many of our friends have moved
to berlin pisa london freo hobart sydney

alice springs canberra
or closer by
closer to the merri or edgars creek theyve moved
to coburg coburg north fawkner reservoir
and now our landlord is dead
and her familys selling
where to now
sophie and i say hmmm
she likes the ocean
i like the creek
dilân likes unicorns
ezgi likes the moon...
as winter approaches
we go to work in the gloom
glooming at work
sitting in traffic
trafficking in shit
who wants to be north for the winter?
oceanic feeling is
being at one with the external world
sensing eternity boundlessness
memory of being newborn and infinite...
more than conjecture
samantha tells me
new research suggests that
water has memory
and i look into her eyes and smile / yes!
berghain is a mythological club in berlin
located in a former thermal plant
and a thermal plant is a power station that

generates electricity and useful heat at
the same time
as many gems move towards coburg north
some coming from brunswick
others from alice springs
our new set of teeth emerges
gums mounted with two rows of cabbage moths
walking right into the demons mouth / a friend
did 50,000 steps in 24hrs
at berghain
then posted his chart
the steps peaking exponentially in hours 21,22,23
he went so hard / high feelings
concrete / techno / and 18m high ceilings
50,000 steps in 86,400 seconds
he grins now
with no eyebrows
laying in tiergarten or mauerpark
all charged up
full of useful heat
electricity
and maybe oceanic feeling
do cats know when theyre about to die?
dont they go hide somewhere to rest in peace?
theres a saying amongst turkish migrants in europe
you depart on the top floor of the plane
and you return in the cargo hold
which is to say repatriated
can i will i be
the other day the kids were stunned

a cat had created a maternity ward below
the deck at ezgis daycare
just before happy mothers day
eight kittens
miao miao she kept saying
my friends therapist said
be a cat
and cats dont count their steps
so now she doesnt wear a bike helmet
recalling a tall man with blond hair
walking towards me / ender /
across the grass at tempelhofer field
offering me a poem for 2 euro
me ordering two
his name was timo dege
and though the ink has faded
i cherish that piece of paper
at work
theres this customer from türkiye
and like many compatriots i get along with
hes a generation older
we zigzag tongues
i think i might be the only worker to serve in another
language here
ne zamandan beri burada çalışıyorsun? he asks
burasi iyi bu işi devam et! he says
he loves it
yes the floors are terrazzo and the range is fantastic
its an institution!
he comes in most days to say hi n snatch a bargain

figure out whose translation of some classical
text is better
he also works at an institution on lygon
walks in on his break dressed in black
carries this enormous presence that makes him
seem seven foot tall instead of six
im still here for my son
he says to me
otherwise id be there
burasi güzel ülke ama...
ive met some nice people here but
ill never have the experiences here
that i had there
we fist bump he smiles
perhaps with reading the answers will reveal themselves
theres a step by step guide to many things in our extended catalogue
7 steps to happy
7 steps to thinking rich
7 steps to creative genius
7 steps to living a grace-filled life...
today i read about an australian sailor rescued at sea
whod set off from baja california aiming for french polynesia
5000kms away
but hit rough seas
living on raw fish and rainwater for 3 months
they rescued him
and asked
why the trip?
and like a tripper he said
*i'm not sure i have the answer to that but i very much enjoy*

*sailing and i love the people of the sea. it's the people of the sea that make us all come together. the ocean is in us. we are the ocean.*
im thinking now of the syrian theatre director
i met in istanbul exiled for putting on a kafka play
his ten siblings now refugees scattered over the world
his 102-year-old father had just moved to
nz to be with one of his daughters...
sophie is in the ocean
and i am too
for a few hours each year
the mexican day of the dead is also
for a few hours each year
a family reunion for the living and the dead too
whose souls visit this world
so leave out some candles some food
sophie says to me
i think weve opened up a can of fish!
7 steps to a confident you
7 steps to self mastery
7 steps to emotional intelligence
7 steps to world revival
they say you dont really belong to a country
until you bury
a loved one in its soil
7 steps to raising amazing children
7 steps to a better portfolio
7 steps to entrepreneurial victory
your perfect dog in 7 steps
neil armstrong reckons he said 'a'

but in the tape you couldnt hear it
so nasa did an audio analysis and found evidence
that he did say it
and so it goes
dilân lost her first two teeth while we
were in türkiye last year
i wondered whether we had assimilated the tooth fairy
or was it somehow universal
and when i asked a turkish friend he said that
when he lost teeth he was told to throw it over
the balcony and yell out
one dirty tooth for you
one pearl tooth for me
which meant a rat would bring you a shiny new one
which led me online to someones phd thesis
on turkish dental folklore
you know
my friend luca returned to
pisa after 12 years in melbourne
his son lupo born here and now in school there
as a kid i never felt there was a chance we would reverse
it back to türkiye
it was almost taboo
but what went on in the deep of my parents mind
ill never know and
now that theyre retiring
things are surfacing
the old country appears
like an octopus on a rock
and we say nasılsın?

7 golden steps to a lasting marriage
7 steps to healing from a toxic relationship
7 step mindset makeover: refocus your thoughts and take charge of your life
windows 7 step-by-step
the great poet of the central anatolian steppe
rumi says
*why plague your heart with indecision?*
*your heart is your pulpit and throne.*
*don't step down.*
*intelligence is your crown.*
*only gems drawn from the depths of you*
*can adorn this crown.*
*gather them.*
dilân finds a small metallic beaded chain
the kind that attaches tags to clothes
and places it between her lower teeth and lip
dad ive decided to get braces!
and she goes to school like that
great! i say amazed / worried about rust
and never hear about it again
my anneanne whos 86 says
hayat ne çabuk harcadın beni
life how quickly youve spent me
all those heartbeats
sharktooth necklace palpitations
they say berghain is a safe space
where people can be whoever they want to be
but thats a myth
capital

feasts on the carcass of
subversion
where community and friendship and
camaraderie goes to die
you just know someones gonna open a 24/7 powerstation
in coburg
and call it coberghain
overlooking the creek
treadmills and mirrors
come get your steps in
buy a drink
keep your air miles down
berlins a state of mind
as sydney road leads to sydney
karl-marx-allee leads to karl marx
the wattles are out on the merri creek
the magpie is warbling
our blood orange is fruiting and
two heaving mandarin trees are popping down the street
one behind a locked gate fruit to ground
the other hangs over two driveways
sophie reaches up and picks a few
theyre small and tasty
i go back with ezgi on my chest
stuff my hat with fruit
the tvs on in the trunkside house
other side of the fence a woman appears
and i say
hope you dont mind that im picking these
go for your life she says

as we walk back home
i peel and hand them to ezgi
she loves it
offers them back to me
i smile
she smiles
i hold them up to the light to check for pips
she holds them up to the sun to check for pips
later
we are sitting on the floorboards
i play her a song
she crawls up to me
pulls up to her feet
rocks bobs grins stumbles
tries again
        tries again
                tries again
first step
1 step

## Our Neighbours Poem

our neighbours face appears above the fence – hello. our neighbours have a chat with us. our neighbours learn our names. our neighbours become our friends. our neighbours landlord thinks the market is ripe. our neighbours are told to leave. our neighbours try to buy their house at an exorbitant price to keep their kids in the school zone. our neighbours are denied. our neighbours move out. our neighbour paul calls me paul, our neighbour paul calls our other neighbour paul too. our neighbour cuts our grass, dumps the leftovers into our messy yard, leaves a bag of toys on our doorstep. our neighbours lend us a shovel we keep and lend out ourselves. our neighbours lend us a blender, give us kids clothes, and say to me – how are you? you look tired. our neighbour gives me fifty bucks to cut her grass and trim her hedges, invites me in for lemonade and tv, the tennis is on. our neighbour sings along in italian on saturday mornings and says – how are you darlin, buutifuu gerl! to my daughter. our neighbour has been in her house 55 years, raised her kids here, worked in a factory, her husband a waiter on lygon st, he died, his pin-up girl posters still hang in their garage, i use his tools, the roads were dirt when they moved in, she doesnt like our paperbark tree and says – dis tree noh gudt! too much messy! because her backyard is paved and she tires of sweeping the leaves up – ill speak to our landlord i say. our neighbours have a whatsapp group. our neighbours have dinner together on the nature strip. our neighbour is a dog sitter and breeder who yells a lot, the dogs howl into the night, she doesnt like how ive parked my car and i dont like how she speaks to me, we arent cordial. our neighbours are watching neighbours on tv. our neighbours are learning piano, its greensleeves waltzing matilda coldplay, now theyre learning trombone too, their plum tree hangs over the fence and we eat the fruit. our neighbours are home. our neighbour climbs the wobbly fence and wants to chat, tomorrow is her tenth birthday – double digits! i say. our neighbour goes away and we water their plants and when we go away they water ours. our neighbour is missing, we hear she has cancer, has chemo, we are fingers crossed. our neighbour is on the roof doing repairs and is peering into our yard, sometimes hes up there because he has a telescope. our neighbour doesnt have a name. our neighbour is in the scouts, helps me break into our house when im locked out without a shirt on, the wind slammed me out, together we finesse the window open, i give her a boost, shes 9, she climbs right in. our neighbour is going camping, is packing their car, pulling a rope, truckies knot, loaded roof racks. our neighbour has chronic pain, is in and out of hospital, is often in bed. our neighbour says – if you need a babysitter im good with kids – and invites us over for dinner, her front door is always open and our daughter runs in to play dress-ups, piano, and feed the chickens. our neighbour is 26 and our daughter is 2 and they are best friends. our neighbour pours us a drink, brings us cake, introduces us to her parents. our neighbour walks into our backyard. our neighbours rhubarb plant is relocated into our veggie patch and does well. our neighbours wheelbarrow is made of plastic. our neighbours chickens get mauled by foxes and we explain this to our kid. our neighbours lend us a hiking pack and walking poles. our neighbour is a musician, gives us their cd and when theyre away, their back window is open and i climb in and borrow their guitar. our neighbours sit in their front yard, the sign of a good share house our neighbours wife dies, he comes fishing with us, lets us cook for him, has a separate washing machine to tenderise octopus, he is 90 now and says – you like cetrioli? – and i say – yes! – not knowing what it is and he gives me four cucumbers in a plastic bag. our neighbour says – i know you like a hot chilli, heya tayk it! our neighbour hits puberty, gets a dog, the dog gets pregnant, the dog goes away to give birth. our neighbour kisses her boyfriend after school in the park and i see them. our neighbour takes long service leave, helps me cut a tree branch, shares their preferred pronouns. our neighbour lends our neighbour a mulcher and together we mulch and talk in between the searing noise. our neighbours are having a bbq, its a birthday party, they let us know beforehand. our neighbours have a trampoline in their front yard. our neighbour grows shrubs and flowers on her nature strip, everyone who comes by is impressed. our neighbours house is full of vintage textiles. our neighbour watches traffic go by, puts witches hats on the street in front of their house, washes all the cars in the neighbourhood for 30 bucks each, hes a hustler, gets a lift off me, brings me a bucket of m&ms, says – nice day! – says – you car look dirty! says – you work late today!? – says – you bring me some of that turkish bread, ok!? – our neighbour drives an uber he keeps immaculately clean. our neighbour says – what can you do i no complain! our neighbour asks me to be a reference for her visa application. our neighbour has loud sex. our neighbour has raucous parties, drum n bass from midday friday till sunday afternoon. our neighbour runs down the stairwell without saying hi, is an overworked teacher. our neighbour waters their balcony plants and it dribbles onto my head as i hang the clothes. our neighbour doesnt bring their bins in. our neighbours waters break. our neighbours pipes burst. our neighbour brings our bins in. our neighbour parks in our car spot. our neighbour leaves boxes of cosmetics on the footpath and we take some body oil. our neighbours are ripping bongs, are gaming, are squatters. our neighbour owns our house, subdivided and built a fortress next door. our neighbour has two cars, a lambikini and a commodore, takes me for a ride in the commodore to his warehouse full of pinball machines and a '57 Chevy to find spare keys in metal drawers after a gust of wind locks me out. our neighbour pours his heart out to me in the car, says – my lifes gone to shit bro, my dad died, my mum died, my woman betrayed me – he misses his mum, i put my hand on his shoulder, he has his exs stuff in garbage bags in the back seat, he talks fast, drives reckless, likes speed. our neighbour doesnt respond to our texts, were having a party and want his blessing, later his family arrive dressed in black. our neighbours are buddhist monks, have a high brick fence. our neighbours stop to chat when we sit on our front lawn. our neighbours give us lemons. our neighbour lets me into her house after ive locked myself out, has many erotic sculptures, gives me tea and biscuits before i jump the fence. our neighbour has lived here 57 years, is deaf, we crank the music higher. our neighbour was my housemate who moved out to move in with her boyfriend a few doors down. our neighbours and i make ice cream. our neighbours sister has just moved to melbourne. our neighbours sister wants to come over for a drink. our neighbours sister knocks on the door and i open it, i say – hello, come in, do you want a drink? our neighbour has a garage sale and i buy their shirt. our neighbour finds a scrunched-up piece of paper hurled over the fence by our other neighbour that reads – have a good party, enjoy yourselves, enjoy your youth, fuck everything that moves!!! our neighbour is a widow whose husband taught my mum at school. our neighbour stands outside and watches the street go by, sometimes he carries home a slab of VB on his shoulder. our neighbour has a baby, has another baby, has a third baby. our neighbour has a sign on their fence that reads – no to inappropriate developments. our neighbour tests the market, sells their house, buys their house, rents their house, renovates their house, demolishes their house, develops the land, builds units, sells the units, keeps one for themselves. our neighbour makes the money. our neighbour bangs on the floorboards when i play music. our neighbour smiles her golden tooth. our neighbour stays up late smoking on their balcony. our neighbour is a bakery. our neighbour takes in the delivery guy quickly. our neighbour is a police station. our neighbour is a house of students. our neighbour is my best friend now. our neighbour and i kiss after pot-luck dinner. our neighbour and i play soccer together, she puts her hand on my thigh in the back of a taxi. our neighbour offers me a ciggie, pours us some wine. our neighbour lays in bed while i make breakfast. our neighbour is in the shower, walks out wet. our neighbour is a doctor. our neighbour doesnt know that i jumped the fence to get my ball and their dog bit me. our neighbour borrows our surfboard. our neighbour becomes leader of the greens. our neighbour is an electrician, calls me boy. our neighbour knocks on the door to play with me and my mum says no, probably because hes a bit older and rides a bmx with a low seat and has a rats tail. our neighbours dont share a fence with us. our neighbours house smells like cigarettes, like curry, like roast, like a chip shop. our neighbours are celebrating ramadan and the street is full of cars. our neighbour collects triumph cars in their yard. our neighbours are greek. our neighbours are macedonian, we are not, but my parents say we understand one another anyway. our neighbours have me over, give me lifts to school, their daughter is a year older than me and i love her. our neighbours let me jump the fence and play footy cricket soccer and basketball, their grandma lives with them, they give me yum lebanese food, we make tapes on their stereo, throw water bombs.

our neighbours dad works night shift in the tyre factory so we gotta be quiet. our neighbour jump starts our car. our neighbour waves to us. our neighbour brings over clothes when i am born. our neighbours say hello.

## Phar Lap

we have a horse in our shed dad
look dad me and gabe are feeding him grass
he likes grass
he eats grass and chaff dad
gabe said his name is phar lap dad
come on phar lap! i got some grass for yoooou!
time to eat up!
its phar laps birthday dad!
can we make phar lap a horse cake dad?
happy birthday phar lap!
lets sing happy birthday to phar lap
lets make phar lap a horse cake out of grass
dad can you hold the cake up to the window?
blow it out phaaaar laaaap!
what noises do horses make dad?
pbrbbrrrrhh ne-he-he-he-hey
happy birth-neigh! thats funny
phaaar laap! pbrbbrrrrhh
whaaaat? i didnt know phar lap was a famous horse
is phar lap dead now dad?
this is phar laps kid
hes also called phar lap
was phar lap a boy or a girl dad?
this is a girl phar lap
she lives in our shed and she runs at night
are you playing a song about phar lap dad?
why did you just put on this song dad?

why did they write a song about phar lap?
phar lap was very fast wasnt he dad?
people love phar lap dont they?
how old was phar lap when he died dad?
like me im almost 5 and a half
he was just little he was just a kid
is that old for a horse dad?
was phar lap alive when you were a kid dad?
was phar lap alive when frida kahlo was alive?
wow thats a long time ago
why did phar lap die dad?
why dad? why was he poisoned?
where did phar lap live?
where was he born?
why did he go to america?
was it like when frida kahlo went to america?
whats a career dad?
how did he get to australia?
like when we went on the spirit of tasmania?
how did he get to america?
did his mum and dad go with him?
did it take more than one whole day and night?
did ruby the 13-year-old rider go with him?
did phar lap have an owner dad?
whats a wealthy industrialist? whats capitalism?
why do horses work dad?
how many races did phar lap win?
wwooooowww 37 thats a lot of races!
why did they call him big red dad?
i like chestnut colour

is my hair a little bit chestnut colour like mums hair dad?
lots of people loved phar lap didnt they?
how do you know so much about phar lap dad?
whats wikipedia?
do you still like horse racing dad?
why dad?
phar lap makes me happy dad
i love phar lap
where is phar lap now dad?
can we go see phar lap?
can we go to the melbourne museum?
can i touch phar lap?
how do they get him to stand up all day?
phar laps really tall dad
phar laps a chestnut
are we dreaming dad?
its like hes alive but hes dead
is this really phar lap?
i love phar lap dad
i love you phar lap
i love you dilân

**A Big Cedar Tree**

rumi says
*don't come without a drum*
*we are celebrating*
*rise and beat the drum!*
*we have triumphed.*
at my cousins wedding
i see ania in the eyes of the drummers
young lebanese bros spirited and irresistible
they bounce and shimmy and drum
dum tak tak dumm tak
dum tak tak dumm tak
dum tak tak dumm tak
my cousin is ~~australian~~
half turkish half lebanese
dum tak tak dum tak
her husband is ~~australian~~
half greek half italian
dum tak dum tak
this is an ~~australian~~ wedding
yeah
led by the luminous wedding singer
a big lebanese cedar tree
asalaam alekum
with a white denim jacket impeccable teeth and gelled curls
hes the best in the business we are told
and the drummers serve him
to elevate us

hes the shaman we need
in this troubled demokrasi
he takes us up
to take us back
to allow us
to see ahead
and it is good for now
this ritual
and rest assured says the mc
each tradition will be represented in song
as the ecstatic sonic east charges the yarra valley vines
each in their own time
a greek zeibekiko in 9/8
an italian tarantella in 6/8
a turkish çiftetelli in 8/4
a lebanese dabke in 4/4
i tremble / i laugh / i tear up
as we call on the past
and the singer stands tall and gets taller as the show goes on
tall and taller
tall enough to open the sky for us
tall now like anias father in poland
once the tallest man in the world she said
then made small here
now bon jovi is demanded
and the singer vanishes
oooooooh were halfway there
oooohh ohh lebanon a prayer
and just like that we are back down to the here & now
two nights earlier the henna night

my cousin sits wearing a red velvet gown passed down
and a veil too
as the women in my family hold candles and circle her twice
my grandma sits beside her and sings
yüksek yüksek tepelere ev kurmasınlar
to make my cousin cry
but instead
she cries
my cousin doesnt speak much turkish
my grandmother no speak much english
but everything is understood
henna is applied to my cousins palm and then to everyone elses
my cousin has been given away
ania asked a lot about my past
to her i came from the land of rumi
that was my treasure
and she was glad to hear i visited his tomb
but have you read him? she asked
now ive read him ania! ive read gold
and when she went to see whirling dervishes in prahran
she was overcome
an ancestral pang
the spiritual deep down the line
and now that ania is no longer
alive
rumi says
*don't grieve. anything you lose comes round in another form...*

## Old Friends

whenever my car needs work my dad comes along
we drive through the suburbs towards our mechanic
today we drive past my old school
you should go back there one day and
say hello he says
introduce yourself
to who baba? i say
while i see the jaunts of my teens
the scenes of my attempts to kiss
he sees the footy grounds of my youth
its good to reminisce he says
yeah i say
do you remember
broken ribs at aberfeldie
broken finger at taylors lakes
concussion and five goals at keilor
four goals in a winning grand final at windy hill
hey remember i took a screamer before the brawl at westmeadows
and kicked a goal on my left foot before
the game got called off
those were good times he says
i know baba
you should catch up with your old footy mates
your school friends too
you have your differences now but theyre your old friends
i dunno baba what would we talk about?
dont think youre better than them

im not but ive moved on baba
its good to reminisce he says...
20 year high school reunion coming up
and nobody i ask thinks i should go
me neither
i dont mention it to my parents tho
60 bucks for canapés! its pricey to reconnect...
old friends are back in town now
from early sharehouse days
its saturday night
we leave dilân with my folks
pull the child seat out of the car
theres five of us driving out to footscray
im stoked to find a car park easy
look up to the sign
no restrictions! yes!
we walk slowly through the mall
making sweet talk / joking around
looking for a place to eat
sophie locks in on a vietnamese place ⅔ full
humble so you know its good
the two women serving appearing to do it all
they prefer we order with numbers
andrew gets the pork belly and the pizzle soup
tara and sophie get the special fried rice
me and lou get the phō
we dont know what pizzle is yet
so i google it
we also get three colour drinks
and a communal pancake

i tip too much chilli oil into the phō
and start to hiccup
the pork belly arrives glistening
pizzle is another word for penis
viet soap on the tv and mirrors
we talk of jobs relationships and flight prices
i tell the story ive been telling everyone of
an acid trip a gremlin and a cash reward
we split the bill effortlessly
now were strolling again
past a man on a bench smoking a ciggi like a flute
a guy in a store amidst fruit boxes filled with phone bits and $20 notes
a 24hr gym with no one
i offer everyone fishermans friends
original flavour
roll past the old irl infoshop
we pursue the call of techno in the air
beyond the train station
bodies bouncing behind temp fencing / heaving
once upon a time we all agree we
wouldve jumped the fence and taken our chances
sophie rolled her ankle once doing that and tara remembers
the dj cuts the bass now and then drops it back in
the crowd goes berserk
sophie rants about it / doesnt like it when i do it at home
play with my mixer like im basic
but i like repetition i cry
we line up at the hyped sorbet place
the queue barely moves in half an hour
maybe the queue is the event

maybe life is a queue
no music inside just a little chatter
we might be the oldest people here
or the weakest bladders here
showing middle-aged tendencies
we analyse their serving system
looking for inefficiencies
yet our annoyance is preliminary
we have admiration for the workers on a go-slow
are unsure of their intent
i wonder if theyre organising or would be open to it
non-stop for two years ive talked union business with friends
now we eye some players trying to ghost ahead in line
but mainly we wonder if this dissociative vibe
is another hallmark of the next generation and
whether this can be a form of rebellion
an alternative or a complement to the bass drop
all this time also allows for a pondering of flavour choices
the arrangement of fruit sugar and cream
one two scoops or three?
what does it say about you
we wear masks in the store
then lick and bite each others cones
walking back up the mall and towards franco cozzos
furniture baron and tv icon
pioneered speaking greek n italian on ads
lou and andrew have seen the doco on him that just dropped
the majesty of this place is debilitating
its grotesqueness
the gaze is always one of outrage and desire

we hate it but we want it
lou says the furniture pieces
the beds the cupboards are ten or twenty grand a piece
not just old wogs buyin up
but some of her trendy friends
we ask tara for opinion / an interior architect
theres a bullethole in the glass window
theyve moved a cabinet over to cover the damaged wall
we enjoy the mural on the side street
franco as deity over an electric sea
trees are bursting up in saline conditions
presumably to be cut down for more furniture
now a couple crosses the road without looking
one wearing vinyl pants that glisten like andrews pork belly
apparently the pizzle soup was not yum
back in the car lou requests classic tunes for our ritual
sing-a-long
like always its hit machine 10 (1995) out of the glovebox
i take us the long way outta footscray
in WA they call this a bog lap
tara lou and sophie from perth
order one
we shove the cd in
shy guy comes on / the bad boys soundtrack
sophie is vibing / rolling her shoulders
tara begins to giggle her famous giggle
lou with her great voice
love and devotion comes on
lou tara sophie and i sing along
andrew not so much / a couple years younger

the real mccoy the first album i ever bought
*tonight is the night /*
*when loves shines so bright /*
*and we will be reunited…*
i know the rap in this song too
the guy with the deep voice
we are coming up up up now as i take us down dynon rd
towards north melb
strike – you sure do / comes on
sophie claims this as the apex of 90s dance music
bright synths fat bassline big breakdown positive vibes
its 1030 and we should be heading to the club
next on is
herbie – right type of mood
herbie as a euphonic genius
shouting MISTER MAGOO!
film clip partially computer-generated
a truly bizarre chart topper
a certified gold record in australia
shipped 35,000 units
one of them mine
released on my tenth birthday
we are yelling now / the car is rocking
rage and video hits flowing through us
nostalgia hits the vein
as we drive along vic market
so many skyscrapers
designed to glisten like pork belly
theres not enough sand in the world for all that concrete
and purple glass

the car is big enough for five
but small enough for us all to be close
i ambush them
even a 2003 subaru impreza with factory speakers
can manage a bass drop
i bring it back in again
my crowd goes nuts
sophie in tears laughing her best laugh
the one that goes hyuh hyuh hyuh from the belly
now were at the big roundabout
and instead of royal parade i take us to carlton
flip it back a notch with m-people
we search for the hero inside ourselves
the crowd suddenly self-aware / unsure
wanted to keep the tempo / the mania
but now all aboard the ballad
taking us up rathdowne and to
48 amess st carlton north
where we all met
i moved in with lou eleven years ago
first kissed sophie on the living room carpet ten years ago
everyone else had gone to bed
now its jodeci – freak n you
a slow jam / pretty sexy
you should name your next kid jodeci lou says
i sing it to sophie now
*everytime i close my eyes*
*i wake up feeling soooo h…*
we turn back onto lygon
scatman john comes on

hes a really talented musician andrew says
if the scatman can do it so can you
is the most inspirational line of the 90s i say
he didnt just overcome his stutter
he rose with it to glory in his 50s and then
departed the realm of the living
having touched millions...
on sydney rd now its tina arena – heaven help my heart
only now are the others truly aware
that this is one enormous bog lap
that wed been in the car roaming for over an hour now
the ride / is the club
the ride / is the joy
the ride / is all
every time we begin to fall
the music picks us back up
the lack of enthusiasm for tina arena reverses
the j.farnham-like propulsive ballad begins to pop
and hum
it unites us in one voice
i pull up in front of jewell station
we all get out / i leave the car running
stereo on the doors remain open
im on the bonnet
ghost riding the whip
corona – try me out / pumping
i finally climb down
we embrace
old friends

## Lion Kink

he was known for placing his head
inside the jaws of a wild cat
that was isaac von something
and queen victoria loved him
like she loved her empire for
terrorising i mean civilising i mean
plundering the world
and as i pour two cups of tea
thanks must go to the workers of the world
to the workers of sri lanka
its mum and me in her backyard
im thursdad / shes semi-retired
ezgis asleep inside
two doves watch on from up high
in their carport nest
at first my dad fed them but
more rushed in
shat everywhere
he panicked / stopped for a bit / felt bad
put out the seeds again
theyre softening as they age / my parents
one of the doves even
walked into the house
and mum said
emily! what are you doing in here?
not everything has to be useful
not everyone can be useful

even angels are working in call centres
even placentas become jontys doulas tapenade
imagine!
200 million musketeers
200 million pamphleteers
200 million volunteers
200 million chocolatiers
200 million gondoliers
200 million overcome fears
200 million non-crocodile tears
200 million billy shakespeares
so
from each according to ability
to each according to need
inequality
is a lions jaw
the rich dwell inside and
push it wider before...snap!
under threat
there will be a moment you
reach into your pocket
and you dont wanna come up empty
a note a charm a knife
some courage-maker
some theory
maybe a mantra
our skills pay their bills
we live for the horizon
the spectre that haunts
if we are lucky / elders have shown the way

if we are lucky / we got teachers and comrades
a tradition passed down generations
like worm grunting for example
a technique used to attract
worms to the surface
to be plucked for fishing bait
some grunters have now turned pro
gaining permits in many locations cos
the government wants a cut and
the empire wants a trophy
lets consider mysore south india 1782
tipu sultan was given a tiger
a life-size semi-automatic big cat
sculpted of wood
depicted in the act of mauling
a european soldier lying on its back
an organs concealed in the tigers body
you turn the handle
the dying soldier moans
later tipu was killed
the city was looted
and *tippoos tiger* got caged in a london musuem
its still there / you visit it / maybe turn the handle
the tiger raaaaarrrgghh
the soldier aaaarrrrgghh
ezgis biting dilân
aaaarrrrgghh
sophie runs to split them up / then me too
hugs n kisses first / logic later
teeth marks on her finger

two cries for help
oh to be a tear across those cheeks
raaaarrrrgghh
in werner herzogs film grizzly man
a couple living amongst brown bears in alaska
are finally eaten by one while filming
the audios preserved and a grim herzog
listens back to it for us
headphones on and says
ohhhww noooooh...
in studs terkels book – working
a worker at the ford plant says
*the first thing they try to do*
*is break your spirit*
almost every turk in broady worked
at ford
my uncles my dede
ford shut down / offshored / hows our spirit?
its hard for me to say
it hard for me to cry
shes never seen me cry
but shes seen me yawn
a tear buds and falls
and ezgi asks
whatsh dat dadda?
my tear
whiii?
first time going overseas
saying goodbyes
mums crying / pins an evil eye

to my pocket
just above the bumbag beneath my shirt
im spirited / away / to LA
at the airport i give a man a five buck
tip!
for providing directions
how sweet / i was
thaaankkyouu brutha!
its 2.19am and ezgis awake
for the leo full moon
august baby now 2½
great mane of hair
people want to touch it but
she roars she awes she bites
you have to win her trust first
go to sleep my little cub
but shes
up up up and awake
and so are we
and she sings
zoom zoom zoom were going to the moon
zoom zoom zoom were going very soon
if u wanna take a trip climb up on my rocket ship
zoom zoom zoom were going to the moon
iiiiiin five fohr free twoooooooo wuuuun!
im sorry for the state of my car
my friend says as she zips thru the gears
overtakes undertakes
no worries i say / i love it
and i say

ive been thinking bout how you
ride your bike no helmet
cos your therapist said
be a cat
and my friend smiles
her car is purring
thrilling hooning up
sydney rd on a sunday night
in a 2000 ford festiva
have you ever read the kids book wild?
youll love it she says
and i do and i do...
everyone wants sweetness
without the calories
sex without
the body
lions
but only in cages...
heres my essay
ender on gender
women cant come
men cant cry
perfect blue spring morning
on dads boat
on the bay
the water is like glass
but in turkish is like clotted cream
kaymak gibi
cos everything comes back to food
first rule / no bananas on board

sophie hands ezgi a carrot stick
tooo noysie! she complains
so we cut the engine and drift for squid
cast out two jigs
my dad hooks one
reels it in
it shoots ink towards the boat
as he lifts it out the water
grabs it beneath the eyes and asks me
should i chop it / to kill it humanely?
once upon a time
we would slay the lamb
now we pay the butcher
i hesitate
put it in the bucket for now i say
we cover it with a towel
dilân watches
ezgis breastfeeding
what? dilân asks
i look to sophie
dede wants to kill the next one quickly i say
so it doesnt suffer
is this one dead?
not yet
now dilân hooks one
reels it in
dad grabs it lowers it chops it above the eyes
WHACK! the colour drains
thats good! dilân says
sorry squidy! dilân says

a stubborn and rebellious son
a newly formed family unit
where theres a will theres always a testament
new funding has poured into the organisation!
this is a day of great jubilation!
this is a jubilee!
silver ruby golden diamond sapphire platinum
whats more than that?
grandparents 65 years in union now departed
grandparents 72 years in union and counting...
during the war against germany
under immense pressure
the british monarchy rebranded
the house of saxe-coburg and gotha
with two lions on the coat of arms
became the house of windsor
purging the family of its german titles
while king georges first cousin tsar nick
was forced to abdicate the throne of russia
raising the spectre of a post-monarchic europa...
on new years night
we are away
adults drinking
six kids at the table gobbling up spagbol
the five year old says
the only meat i like is sausage
the nine year old says
i only like cow as cheese but
ill eat chicken if i have to
and dilân the six year old says

i love lamb
but i love to eat them
but i dont really like / i mean
i love the taste of them
but i dont like eating them...
at night she sleeps with her
number 1 soft toy
lamby the lamb
we understand...
he was 97 but
prince philip didnt flip his car
we did...
the night after fishing
we eat calamari for dinner
light streams in hitting the glass jug
on wobbly table
a shimmer on the wall
like the glimmer of the jig beneath yesterdays sea
ezgi points to it and says oooooh
and i say something about the motion of the water
and she rolls it around her mouth
moh-shun moh-shun moh-shun
and then she says / i wanna go zoo
ok i say lets go next week
i wanna see a horse dada
oh ok / do they make motion?
yaa dada
there are no horses in the zoo i say
whiii? asks ezgi
why baba? asks dilân

zoos are for wild animals i say
and most horses arent wild
cos theyre broken in
cos theyre made to work...
she comes from a verbacious family so
im shocked to hear that
sophie has never heard the phrase
robbing peter to pay paul
but thats probably just cos
her dads name is peter...
were playing but ive gotta go to the kitchen
ill be back i say
in a jiffy
a jiffy? dilân grins
how longs that?
a very short time i say
like one minute?
like one second?
maybe 1/100th of a second i say
like tstt or cht she asks?
way shorter i say
different fields have assigned various
units of measurements to jiffy!
like engineers
chemists
and astrophysicists
but youre a poet daaad
exactly i say
we keep it versatile and immense
come on kids lets brush teeth and put on shoes

were late for school!!!
but daaad i dont wanna go to school todaaaay!
my friend said army service was good / for him
cos he learnt to get up shower shave get dressed
and make his bed in fifteen minutes
my kids are conscientious objectors
theyre getting trained for other fronts
archaeology is a new interest
dilân was given a slab of soft stone
filled with gems
did you know
in the uk they excavated lion fossils
680,000 years old!
in the book – wild
a baby is raised by animals in the forest
hunters abduct her
doctors examine her
teachers discipline her
they try to brush her hair
dress her
get her on time
but she rages / tears up the place
breaks out and returns to the forest
dilân and i read it over and over
the animals are her parents so
shes not human dilân says
i think shes human i reply but
we could argue why that is...
the last lion tamer in
britain was refused a licence

cos hed already lost an arm
the british mens national football team
is nicknamed
the three lions
and the womens is
the lionesses
so the british lion industry continues
despite a lack of actual lions
when i read that lions were colonising
much of europe six to eight thousand years ago
i wonder what that means exactly now that
my friend justin has given his cat meadow
to amy
cos he couldnt care for him anymore
and after hiding under a bed for a few days
meadow now roams easy at amys
can a cat feel happiness?
hes happy amy says
shows me a pic of them snuggling in bed...
sophie says she needs a good cry
but she hasnt had the time
and i say im sorry
cos im partly to blame
and how big that part is
we argue over
late at night
but never settle
we just tire
and sometimes
have a cuddle...

my friends a jeweller and made these
figures amulets talismans
for a show and propped them on a window ledge
to take in exchange for a future gift
there was a moon a dog and lots more
i got a scraggly sun with a face
and remembered that bataille said
the sun gives without ever receiving
and the more i look at the charm
the more i see a lion with big hair
thank u naasicaa youve filled my cup
like the wizard who gave the lion
a potion to give him courage
lets drink this wine...
when i was six our fox terrier disappeared
my parents said he ran away
now dilân is six
and she wants a dog to run in
a dog a pony a guinea pig anything
but sophie and i dont want one
we tarry and stake our case
cos our gut says no
and dilân says ooaaaww daaaad
and ezgi says ooaaaww daaadd
and dilân says stop copying me ezgi!
and ezgi says stop copying me ezgi!
have you read the iliad?
have youuuu read the iliad?
lions lived in south europe until the classical period
homer said so 45 times

but was this due to his experience in asia minor...
a magpie / is dying / in the alleyway / at work / is dead
under a wheelie bin / sam and i / watch on
as justin cups it / with a piece a paper / and lifts it
/ into the bin / thats brave / sam says / thats rough / i go / your
cat meadow mighta done this / i say / as a gift
to say dad / goodbye / dont worry dad / its all g...
a survey recently revealed that a slim majority
of uk teenagers
prefer dictatorship to democracy
when people say dogs are needy
do they really mean
require enslavement?
only if our homes are democratic
our workplaces are democratic
our publics are democratic
then can we say we live in a democracy
why? cos i said so!
to lionise means to make someone famous
rage can get to anyone at work
a white tiger named mantacore ended
siegfried & roys career with
one swift blow after
roy had tried to make the tiger say
hello
to the las vegas audience
and mantacore took it personally
severing his bosses spine...
to drive around in a jag / a merc / a maserati
no longer means youre powerful

it means you too mighta been enslaved
fascism is simply the boot of boss-rule
when trickle-down dries up
no wonder the british have a lion kink
big cats as apex as untameable
the wildest of the wild
and when it comes to people
they say
orientals africans indigenous peoples
are meant to be harder to break in
than whites
too different! too wild!
when karl marx visited algeria
before his death
he wrote to his daughter
*inequality is an abomination to a true mussalman*
*but these sentiments will go to rack and ruin*
*without a revolutionary movement!*
you say youre tired
but i open the fridge
my yoghurt contains
50 billion good bacteria
heres a scoop
lets gooooo!!!!
mantacore issued a warning
that goes like this
at your next gathering
dont try to make your kids say hello
to anyone / just lead by example
at the poetry reading in the backyard

ezgi
loves ladybirds so much
she cant help killing them
and she counts the toll
wahn chu free for fii sish sheven ate niiine
chen eleben tchwel firteem
ayteem niiiynteen twemmy!
her new favourite word is
bicosz
aimé césaire said after ww2
that fascism is not
new to europeans but has just debuted
on home soil…
the wood turtle has adapted
to worm charming
they stamp their feet
pat pat pat pat
attracting their prey
to the surface
eat eat eat eat!
the worlds a jungle my dad says
and i try to argue with him
fathers have only interpreted the world
in various ways
the point however is to change it
ok the jungle rocks
this is our
sierra maestra
what are we doing
we are charming

so remember
if they stick their head
into your mouth
make sure
to take
a bite

## Acknowledgements

To Sophie, Dilân and Ezgi, my canıms. I love you.

To Gabe, for your tireless help with these poems and so much more. Comrades in arms.

To Mum, Dad and my entire family. In honour of your endless support and love.

To my friends, you lift me up. Come over!

To my colleagues at Readings but also all my comrades over the years for making the days go by with a laugh.

To Ivor and the team at Giramondo for believing in my work.

To my teachers and fellow students over the years, particularly Ania Walwicz.

To Lucy, π.O. and the poetry community in Melbourne for all the gigs, chats and support.

To Sick Leave, Thin Red Lines, AVANT GAGA, Unusual Work and MSL for giving me a chance to perform earlier versions of these poems.

To the writers, poets, thinkers and artists whose work helped power these poems.

To the Wurundjeri Woiwurring people of the Kulin Nation, on whose lands I live and labour. I pay my respects to you. Sovereignty was never ceded.

Longer quotes in the text have been drawn from the following:

*On Call: Political Essays* by June Jordan. Copyright © 1985 by Christopher D. Meyer. All rights reserved. Reprinted by permission of the Frances Goldin Literary Agency (p. 6).

Nile Rodgers interview by Michael Segalov, *Huck Magazine*, 25 June 2018 (p. 43–44).

*Life's Good, Brother* by Nâzim Hikmet, translated by Mutlu Konuk Blasing, Persea Books, 2013 (p. 69).

Excerpts from *Gold,* Poems by Rumi, Translated by Haleh Liza Gafori, New York Review Books/NYRB Classics, 2022 (p. 97, p. 109, p. 111).

Earlier versions of the following poems have been published in other publications. Thanks goes to everyone working on those journals and anthologies:

'A Workers Paradise', published in *Unusual Work* 35, and *Best of Australian Poems,* 2023.

'In Real Life', published in *Cordite* 106: Open.

'Are You Ready Poem', winner of the 2021 *Overland* Judith Wright Poetry Prize.

'Funk N Wagnalls' and 'Erotics Of Bookselling', published in HEAT Series 3 Number 9.

'Get Your Overalls On', published in *Unusual Work* 37.

'Our Neighbours Poem', published in *Overland on* 3 November 2023, and *Best of Australian Poems,* 2024.

'Phar Lap', published in *Overland* on 25 October 2024.

'A Big Cedar Tree', published in *Lieu Journal* #4: Time Travel (as 'Still arriving in so-called australia').

## About the author

Ender Başkan is a poet and bookseller. His poetry has been published in HEAT, *Overland*, *Meanjin*, *Cordite*, *Unusual Work* and *Best of Australian Poems*. He is the winner of the 2021 Overland Judith Wright Poetry Prize and author of the novel *A Portrait of Alice as a Young Man*. A co-founder of Vre Books press, Agog poetry readings and Study, an experimental space, he lives in Melbourne on Wurundjeri land.